Standards of Practice Handbook

NINTH EDITION

2005

CFA
INSTITUTE

ISBN 1-932495-33-9
Printed in the United States of America
15 June 2005

Contents

Standard VII: Responsibilities as a CFA Institute Member or CFA Candidate

Preface

The purpose of this *Standards of Practice Handbook* (Handbook) is to provide up-to-date guidance to the people who grapple with real ethical problems in the investment profession, where theory meets practice and ethics gain meaning. This Handbook is intended for a diverse and global audience: CFA Institute members navigating ambiguous ethical situations; supervisors and subordinates determining the nature of their responsibilities to one another, to clients and potential clients, and to the securities markets; and candidates preparing for the Chartered Financial Analyst examinations.

Ethics in the Investment Profession

Ethical practices by investment professionals benefit all market participants and stakeholders and lead to increased investor confidence in global capital markets. Clients are reassured that the investment professionals they hire have the clients' best interest in mind and investment professionals benefit from the "reputational capital" such integrity generates. Ethical practices instill a public trust in the fairness of markets, allowing them to function efficiently. In short, good ethics is a fundamental requirement of the investment profession.

An important goal of CFA Institute is to ensure that the organization and its members develop, promote, and follow the highest ethical standards in the investment industry. The CFA Institute Code of Ethics and Standards of Professional Conduct (Code and Standards) are the foundation supporting the organization's quest to advance the interests of the global investment community by establishing and maintaining the highest standards of professional excellence and integrity. The Code of Ethics is a set of principles that define the professional conduct CFA Institute expects from its members and candidates in the CFA Program. The Code works in tandem with the Standards of Professional Conduct which outlines conduct that constitutes fair and ethical business practices.

For more than 40 years, CFA Institute members and candidates in the CFA Program have been required to abide by the organization's Code and Standards. Periodically, CFA Institute has revised and updated its Code and Standards to ensure that they remain relevant to the changing nature of the investment profession and representative of the "highest standard" of professional conduct. As the investment profession evolves, the list of ethical issues lengthens, from personal investing and soft commissions to misleading advice and the need to separate objective analysis from company promotion. New challenges are always emerging. As economies become more sophisticated and interconnected, new investment opportunities are constantly being created, along with new financial instruments to make the most of those opportunities for clients. Although the investment world has become a far more complex place since this Handbook was first published, distinguishing right from wrong remains the paramount principle of the Code of Ethics and Standards of Professional Conduct.

Evolution of the CFA Institute
Code of Ethics and Standards of Professional Conduct

Generally the changes to the Code and Standards, over the years, have been minor. CFA Institute revised the language of the Standards and occasionally tacked on a new standard addressing prominent issues of the day. For instance, in 1992, CFA Institute added the standard addressing performance presentation to the existing list of standards. The last major changes came in 1996 and were mostly structural in nature. CFA Institute organized them to coincide with the constituencies of investment professionals–clients, employers, investors, the public, and the profession.

After a long review process, several revisions, solicitation and careful consideration of public comment from its members, candidates, and investment professionals, CFA Institute has adopted the new and revised version of the Code and Standards included in this book. The changes include a reorganization of the standards, adoption of new standards, and revisions to existing standards. CFA Institute believes that the revisions clarify the requirements of the Code and Standards and effectively convey to its global membership what constitutes "best practice" in a number of areas relating to the investment profession.

These new standards are effective 1 January 2006. CFA Institute has published this 9th edition of the *Standards of Practice Handbook* to offer guidance, interpretation, applications, and recommended procedures for compliance for the new standards.

Summary of Changes

Reorganization of Standards. The organization of past versions of the Standards were based on the CFA Institute member or candidate's responsibilities to various constituencies: the public, the client, the employer, and the profession. This led to the repetition of concepts in an attempt to fit broad substantive ideas into specific categories even though those ideas have general application. For example, disclosure of conflicts of interest was addressed in two separate standards, one dealing with disclosure of conflicts to employers, the other dealing with disclosure of conflicts to clients. Also, misrepresentation was addressed in several standards relating to investment recommendations, performance and credentials. Multiple references to similar ideas detracted from clarity and comprehension of the ethical concepts contained in the Code and Standards.

The revised Standards are organized by topic to streamline the structure and improve comprehension. Instead of five standards that discuss member and candidate conduct as it relates to various groups, the new Standards are organized into seven general topics:

I. Professionalism
II. Integrity of Capital Markets

III. Duties to Clients
IV. Duties to Employers
V. Investment Analysis, Recommendations, and Action
VI. Conflicts of Interest
VII. Responsibilities as CFA Institute Members or CFA Candidates

Revising Current Standards. CFA Institute has expanded the Standards (e.g., misrepresentation, duty to employer, suitability, duty of loyalty to clients, disclosure of conflicts, and material nonpublic information) to better address the state of the investment profession and establish clear "best practices" in these areas.

Clarifying Requirements. In some instances, the guidance in prior versions of the Handbook included "requirements" with which all members and candidates had to comply, even though this conduct was not specifically set forth in the Standards themselves. For example, the prior guidance prohibited acceptance of gifts over a specific dollar amount, even though the specific prohibition was not found in the Standards. CFA Institute has eliminated or incorporated these requirements into the new Standards as appropriate so that members and candidates are clearly on notice about what conduct the Code and Standards requires or prohibits. The guidance included in the 9th edition of the Handbook expands on the requirements set forth in the Code and Standards and does not introduce new requirements.

New Standards. CFA Institute added standards relating to market manipulation and record retention to better address the state of the investment profession and establish clear "best practices" in these areas.

Eliminating the Requirement to Inform Employers of the Code and Standards. Previously the Standards of Professional Conduct included a requirement that members and candidates notify their employer of their responsibility to abide by the Code and Standards. Although it is in the member or candidate's best interest to notify their employer, and thereby potentially avoid being placed in a compromising position, CFA Institute believes that notification should be a recommendation rather than a requirement in the Standards. Such a recommendation is included in the Preamble to the Code of Ethics.

Maintaining Relevance to a Global Membership. In some areas (e.g., use of material nonpublic information and fiduciary duty) the prior versions of the Code and Standards were based on U.S. law and regulation and no longer reflected best practice in the global investment industry. Therefore, CFA Institute has revised the Standards to make them less U.S.-centric to maintain the highest ethical standard on a global basis.

Text Revisions. As the investment industry and, as a result, CFA Institute membership has become more global, it is critical for the Code and Standards to use language that, to the extent possible, can be easily understood and translated into different languages. Therefore, in some instances CFA Institute has eliminated, modified, or added language for clarity, even though it is not the intent to change the meaning of a particular provision.

Changes to the Code and Standards have far reaching implications for CFA Institute membership, the CFA Program, and the investment industry as a whole. Unlike other voluntary ethical standards promulgated by the organization through the CFA Centre for Financial Market Integrity (e.g., the GIPS standards, Soft Dollar Standards, Trade Management Guidelines, Research Objectivity Standards, Best Practice Guidelines Governing Analyst and Corporate Issuer Relations, Asset Manager Code of Professional Conduct), members and CFA Candidates are required to adhere to the Code and Standards. In addition, the Code and Standards are increasingly being adopted, in whole or in part, by firms and regulatory authorities. Their relevance goes well beyond CFA Institute members and CFA candidates.

It is imperative that the Code and Standards be updated if they are to be effective and represent the highest ethical standards in the global investment industry. CFA Institute strongly believes that the revisions and reorganization of the Code and Standards are not undertaken for cosmetic change but add value by addressing legitimate concerns and improving comprehension.

Standards of Practice Handbook

The periodic revisions to the Code and Standards have come in conjunction with the update of the *Standards of Practice Handbook*. The Handbook is the fundamental element of the ethics education effort of CFA Institute and the primary resource for guidance in interpreting and implementing the Code and Standards. The Handbook seeks to educate members and candidates on how to apply the Code and Standards to their professional lives and thereby benefit their clients, employers, and the investing public in general. The Handbook explains the purpose of the Standards and how they apply in a variety of situations. The guidance discusses and amplifies each Standard and suggests procedures to prevent violations.

Examples in the "Application of the Standard" section are meant to illustrate how the Standard applies to hypothetical factual situations. The names contained in the examples are fictional and are not meant to refer to any actual person or entity. Unless otherwise stated, individuals in each example are CFA Institute members and/or holders of the Chartered Financial Analyst designation. Because factual circumstances vary so widely and often involve gray areas, the explanatory material and examples are not intended to be all inclusive. Many examples set forth in the Application of the Standard section involve Standards that have legal counterparts; members are strongly urged to discuss with their supervisors and legal and compliance departments the content of the Code and Standards and the members' general obligations under the Code and Standards.

CFA Institute recognizes that the presence of any set of ethical standards can create a false sense of security unless the documents are fully understood, enforced, and made a meaningful part of everyday professional activities. The Handbook is intended to provide a useful frame of reference that lends substance to the understanding of professional behavior in the investment decision-making process. This book cannot cover every contingency or circumstance, and it does not attempt to do so. The development and interpretation of the Code and Standards is an evolving process and will be subject to continuing refinement.

CFA Institute Professional Conduct Program

All CFA Institute members and candidates enrolled in the CFA Program are required to comply with the Code and Standards. The CFA Institute Bylaws and Rules of Procedure for Proceedings Related to Professional Conduct (Rules of Procedure) form the basic structure for enforcing the Code and Standards. The Rules of Procedure are based on two primary principles: (1) fair process to the member and candidate and (2) confidentiality of proceedings. The CFA Institute Board of Governors maintains oversight and responsibility for the Professional Conduct Program (PCP) through the Disciplinary Review Committee (DRC), which is responsible for the enforcement of the Code and Standards.

Professional Conduct staff, under the direction of the CFA Institute Designated Officer, conducts professional conduct inquiries. Several circumstances can prompt an inquiry. Members and candidates must self disclose on the annual Professional Conduct Statement all matters that question their professional conduct, such as involvement in civil litigation, a criminal investigation, or being the subject of a written complaint. Secondly, written complaints received by Professional Conduct staff can bring about an investigation. Third, CFA Institute staff may become aware of questionable conduct by a member or candidate through the media or other public source. Fourth, CFA examination proctors can submit a violation report for any candidate suspected to have compromised his or her professional conduct during the examination.

When an inquiry is initiated, the Professional Conduct staff conducts an investigation that may include requesting a written explanation from the member or candidate; interviewing the member or candidate, complaining parties, and third parties; and collecting documents and records in support of its investigation. The Designated Officer, upon reviewing the material obtained during the investigation, may conclude the inquiry with no disciplinary sanction, issue a cautionary letter, or continue proceedings to discipline the member or candidate. If the Designated Officer finds that a violation of the Code and Standards occurred, the Designated Officer proposes a disciplinary sanction, which may be rejected or accepted by the member or candidate. If the member or candidate rejects the proposed sanction, the matter is referred to a hearing by a panel of CFA Institute members.

Sanctions imposed by CFA Institute may have significant consequences, including condemnation by the sanctioned members' peers and possible ramifications for employment. Candidates enrolled in the CFA Program who have violated the Code and Standards may be suspended from further participation in the CFA program.

Adoption of the Code and Standards

The CFA Institute Code and Standards applies to individual members of CFA Institute and candidates for the CFA designation. However, CFA Institute does encourage firms to adopt the Code of Ethics and Standards of Professional Conduct as part of their firm code of ethics. There are no formal procedures for adopting the Code and Standards but those who claim compliance should fully understand the requirements of the Code and Standards.

Although CFA Institute welcomes public acknowledgement, when appropriate, that firms are using the CFA Institute Code and Standards, no attribution is necessary. For firms that would like to distribute the Code and Standards to clients and potential clients, attractive, one-page copies of the Code and Standards, including translations, are available on the CFA Institute website (www.cfainstitute.org).

CFA Institute, through its CFA Centre for Financial Market Integrity, has also published an Asset Manager Code of Professional Conduct (AMC) that is designed, in part, to assist U.S. firms comply with the regulations mandating codes of ethics for investment advisers. The AMC provides specific, practical guidelines for asset managers in six areas: loyalty to clients, the investment process, trading, compliance, performance evaluation and disclosure. Although the Code and Standards are aimed at individual investment professionals who are members of the CFA Institute or candidates for the CFA designation, the Asset Manager Code of Professional Conduct has been drafted for firms. The AMC is included as an appendix and also can be found on the CFA Website.

CFA Institute encourages firms adopting either the Code and Standards or the Asset Manager Code of Conduct to notify CFA Institute that they have adopted or are incorporating these standards as part of their firm codes of ethics.

Acknowledgements

Because CFA Institute is a volunteer organization, its work to promote ethical practice in the investment profession relies to a great degree on the goodwill of its members to devote their time on the organization's behalf. Such goodwill is also in abundance among CFA Institute members acting in an individual capacity to extend ethical integrity.

The CFA Institute Standards of Practice Council (SPC), a group currently consisting of 15 CFA Charterholder volunteers from nine different countries, is charged with maintaining and interpreting the Code and Standards and ensuring that they are effective. The SPC draws its membership from a broad spectrum of organizations in the securities field, including brokers, investment advisors, banks, and insurance companies. In most instances, the SPC members also have important supervisory responsibilities within their firms.

The SPC continually evaluates the Code and Standards, as well as the guidance in the Handbook, to ensure that they are:

- Representative of the "highest standard" of professional conduct,
- Relevant to the changing nature of the investment profession,
- Globally applicable,
- Sufficiently comprehensive, practical, and specific,
- Enforceable, and
- Testable for the CFA Program.

Over the last two years, the SPC has spent countless hours reviewing and discussing revisions to the Code and Standards and updates to the guidance that makes up this 9th edition of the Handbook. Below is a list of the current members of the SPC who generously donated their time and energy to this effort.

Lee Price, CFA, Chair
Ross E. Hallett, CFA
Samuel B. Jones, CFA
Lynn S. Mander, CFA
Todd P. Lowe, CFA
Sunil Singhania, CFA
Miroslaw Panek, CFA

Mario Eichenberger, CFA
Toshihiko Saito, CFA
Richard Wayman, CFA
Martha Oberndorfer, CFA
Mark Sinsheimer, CFA
Brian O'Keefe, CFA

Finally, this book is dedicated to the late Jules Huot, CFA, a long-time member of the SPC and volunteer for CFA Institute who tirelessly advocated for ethics in the investment profession and constantly worked to promote ethics and integrity within the industry.

CFA Institute Code of Ethics and Standards of Professional Conduct

Preamble to the
CFA Institute Code of Ethics and Standards of Professional Conduct

The CFA Institute Code of Ethics and Standards of Professional Conduct (Code and Standards) are fundamental to the values of CFA Institute values and essential to achieving its mission to lead the investment profession globally by setting high standards of education, integrity, and professional excellence. High ethical standards are critical to maintaining the public's trust in financial markets and in the investment profession. Since their creation in the 1960s, the Code and Standards have promoted the integrity of CFA Institute members and served as a model for measuring the ethics of investment professionals globally, regardless of job function, cultural differences, or local laws and regulations. All CFA Institute members (including holders of the Chartered Financial Analyst® (CFA®) designation) and CFA candidates must abide by the Code and Standards. Violations may result in disciplinary sanctions by CFA Institute. Sanctions can include revocation of membership, candidacy in the CFA Program, and the right to use the CFA designation.

The Code of Ethics

Members of CFA Institute (including Chartered Financial Analyst® [CFA®] charterholders) and candidates for the CFA designation ("Members and Candidates") must:

- Act with integrity, competence, diligence, respect, and in an ethical manner with the public, clients, prospective clients, employers, employees, colleagues in the investment profession, and other participants in the global capital markets.
- Place the integrity of the investment profession and the interests of clients above their own personal interests.
- Use reasonable care and exercise independent professional judgment when conducting investment analysis, making investment recommendations, taking investment actions, and engaging in other professional activities.
- Practice and encourage others to practice in a professional and ethical manner that will reflect credit on themselves and the profession.
- Promote the integrity of, and uphold the rules governing, capital markets.
- Maintain and improve their professional competence and strive to maintain and improve the competence of other investment professionals.

Standards of Professional Conduct

I. PROFESSIONALISM

A. **Knowledge of the Law.** Members and Candidates must understand and comply with all applicable laws, rules, and regulations (including the CFA Institute Code of Ethics and Standards of Professional Conduct) of any government, regulatory organization, licensing agency, or professional association governing their professional activities. In the event of conflict, Members and Candidates must comply with the more strict law, rule, or regulation. Members and Candidates must not knowingly participate or assist in and must dissociate from any violation of such laws, rules, or regulations.

B. **Independence and Objectivity.** Members and Candidates must use reasonable care and judgment to achieve and maintain independence and objectivity in their professional activities. Members and Candidates must not offer, solicit, or accept any gift, benefit, compensation, or consideration that reasonably could be expected to compromise their own or another's independence and objectivity.

C. **Misrepresentation.** Members and Candidates must not knowingly make any misrepresentations relating to investment analysis, recommendations, actions, or other professional activities.

D. **Misconduct.** Members and Candidates must not engage in any professional conduct involving dishonesty, fraud, or deceit or commit any act that reflects adversely on their professional reputation, integrity, or competence.

II. INTEGRITY OF CAPITAL MARKETS

A. **Material Nonpublic Information.** Members and Candidates who possess material nonpublic information that could affect the value of an investment must not act or cause others to act on the information.

B. **Market Manipulation.** Members and Candidates must not engage in practices that distort prices or artificially inflate trading volume with the intent to mislead market participants.

III. DUTIES TO CLIENTS

A. **Loyalty, Prudence, and Care.** Members and Candidates have a duty of loyalty to their clients and must act with reasonable care and exercise prudent judgment. Members and Candidates must act for the benefit of their clients and place their clients' interests before their employer's or their own interests. In relationships with clients, Members and Candidates must determine applicable fiduciary duty and must comply with such duty to persons and interests to whom it is owed.

B. **Fair Dealing.** Members and Candidates must deal fairly and objectively with all clients when providing investment analysis, making investment recommendations, taking investment action, or engaging in other professional activities.

C. **Suitability.**

1. When Members and Candidates are in an advisory relationship with a client, they must:

    a. Make a reasonable inquiry into a client's or prospective clients' investment experience, risk and return objectives, and financial constraints prior to making any investment recommendation or taking investment action and must reassess and update this information regularly.

    b. Determine that an investment is suitable to the client's financial situation and consistent with the client's written objectives, mandates, and constraints before making an investment recommendation or taking investment action.

    c. Judge the suitability of investments in the context of the client's total portfolio.

2. When Members and Candidates are responsible for managing a portfolio to a specific mandate, strategy, or style, they must only make investment recommendations or take investment actions that are consistent with the stated objectives and constraints of the portfolio.

D. **Performance Presentation.** When communicating investment performance information, Members or Candidates must make reasonable efforts to ensure that it is fair, accurate, and complete.

E. **Preservation of Confidentiality.** Members and Candidates must keep information about current, former, and prospective clients confidential unless:

1. The information concerns illegal activities on the part of the client or prospective client,

2. Disclosure is required by law, or

3. The client or prospective client permits disclosure of the information.

IV. **DUTIES TO EMPLOYERS**

A. **Loyalty.** In matters related to their employment, Members and Candidates must act for the benefit of their employer and not deprive their employer of the advantage of their skills and abilities, divulge confidential information, or otherwise cause harm to their employer.

B. **Additional Compensation Arrangements.** Members and Candidates must not accept gifts, benefits, compensation, or consideration that competes with, or might reasonably be expected to create a conflict of interest with, their employer's interest unless they obtain written consent from all parties involved.

C. **Responsibilities of Supervisors.** Members and Candidates must make reasonable efforts to detect and prevent violations of applicable laws, rules, regulations, and the Code and Standards by anyone subject to their supervision or authority.

V. **INVESTMENT ANALYSIS, RECOMMENDATIONS, AND ACTION**

A. **Diligence and Reasonable Basis.** Members and Candidates must:

1. Exercise diligence, independence, and thoroughness in analyzing investments, making investment recommendations, and taking investment actions.

2. Have a reasonable and adequate basis, supported by appropriate research and investigation, for any investment analysis, recommendation, or action.

B. **Communication with Clients and Prospective Clients.** Members and Candidates must:

1. Disclose to clients and prospective clients the basic format and general principles of the investment processes used to analyze investments, select securities, and construct portfolios and must promptly disclose any changes that might materially affect those processes.

2. Use reasonable judgment in identifying which factors are important to their investment analyses, recommendations, or actions and include those factors in communications with clients and prospective clients.

3. Distinguish between fact and opinion in the presentation of investment analysis and recommendations.

C. **Record Retention.** Members and Candidates must develop and maintain appropriate records to support their investment analysis, recommendations, actions, and other investment-related communications with clients and prospective clients.

VI. **CONFLICTS OF INTEREST**

A. **Disclosure of Conflicts.** Members and Candidates must make full and fair disclosure of all matters that could reasonably be expected to impair their independence and objectivity or interfere with respective duties to their clients, prospective clients, and employer. Members and Candidates must ensure that such disclosures are prominent, are delivered in plain language, and communicate the relevant information effectively.

B.   **Priority of Transactions.** Investment transactions for clients and employers must have priority over investment transactions in which a Member or Candidate is the beneficial owner.

C.   **Referral Fees.** Members and Candidates must disclose to their employer, clients, and prospective clients, as appropriate, any compensation, consideration, or benefit received by, or paid to, others for the recommendation of products or services.

VII. **RESPONSIBILITIES AS A CFA INSTITUTE MEMBER OR CFA CANDIDATE**

A.   **Conduct as Members and Candidates in the CFA Program.** Members and Candidates must not engage in any conduct that compromises the reputation or integrity of CFA Institute or the CFA designation or the integrity, validity, or security of the CFA examinations.

B.   **Reference to CFA Institute, the CFA Designation, and the CFA Program.** When referring to CFA Institute, CFA Institute membership, the CFA designation, or candidacy in the CFA Program, Members and Candidates must not misrepresent or exaggerate the meaning or implications of membership in CFA Institute, holding the CFA designation, or candidacy in the CFA program.

Standard I: Professionalism

(A) Knowledge of the Law

Members and Candidates must understand and comply with all applicable laws, rules, and regulations (including the CFA Institute Code of Ethics and Standards of Professional Conduct) of any government, regulatory organization, licensing agency, or professional association governing their professional activities. In the event of conflict, Members and Candidates must comply with the more strict law, rule, or regulation. Members and Candidates must not knowingly participate or assist in and must dissociate from any violation of such laws, rules, or regulations.

Guidance

Members and candidates must have an understanding of applicable laws and regulations of all countries in which they trade securities or provide investment advice or other investment services. This standard does not require members and candidates to become experts in compliance. Investment professionals are not required to have detailed knowledge of or be experts on all laws that could potentially govern the member or candidate's activities. However, members and candidates must comply with the laws and regulations that directly govern their work.

Relationship between the Code and Standards and Local Law. Some members or candidates may live, work, or provide investment services to clients living in a country that has no law or regulation governing a particular action or that has laws or regulations that differ from the requirements of the Code and Standards. When applicable law and the Code and Standards require different conduct, members and candidates must follow the more strict of the applicable law or the Code and Standards.

"Applicable law" is the law that governs the member or candidate's conduct. Which law applies will depend on the particular facts and circumstances of each case. The "more strict" law or regulation is the law or regulation that imposes greater restrictions on the action of the member or candidate or calls for the member or candidate to exert a greater degree of action that protects the interests of investors. For example, applicable law or regulation may not require members and candidates to disclose referral fees received from or paid to others for the recommendation of investment products or services. However, because the Code and Standards impose this obligation, members and candidates must disclose the existence of such fees.

Members and candidates must adhere to the following principles:

- Members and candidates must comply with applicable law or regulation related to their professional activities.
- Members and candidates must not engage in conduct that constitutes a violation of the Code and Standards, even though it may otherwise be legal.
- In the absence of any applicable law or regulation or when the Code and Standards impose a higher degree of responsibility than applicable laws and regulations, members and candidates must adhere to the Code and Standards.

Applications of these principles are outlined in **Exhibit 1**.

CFA Institute members are obligated to abide by the CFA Institute Articles of Incorporation, Bylaws, Code of Ethics, Standards of Professional Conduct, Rules of Procedure for Proceedings Related to Professional Conduct, Membership Agreement, and other applicable rules promulgated by CFA Institute, all as amended from time to time. CFA candidates who are not members must also abide by these documents (except for the Membership Agreement), as well as rules and regulations related to the administration of the CFA examination, the Candidate Responsibility Statement, and the Candidate Pledge.

Participation or Association with Violations by Others. Members and candidates are responsible for violations in which they *knowingly* participate or assist. Although members and candidates are presumed to have knowledge of all applicable laws, rules, and regulations, CFA Institute acknowledges that members may not recognize violations if they are not aware of all the facts giving rise to the violations. Standard I applies when members and candidates know or should know that their conduct may contribute to a violation of applicable laws, rules, regulations, or the Code and Standards.

If a member or candidate has reasonable grounds to believe that imminent or ongoing client or employer activities are illegal or unethical, the member or candidate must dissociate, or separate, from the activity. In extreme cases, dissociation may require a member or candidate to leave his or her employer. However, there are intermediate steps that members and candidates may take to dissociate from ethical violations of others. The first step should be to attempt to stop the behavior by bringing it to the attention of the employer through a supervisor or the compliance department. Members and candidates may consider directly confronting the person or persons committing the violation. If these attempts are unsuccessful, then members and candidates have a responsibility to step away and dissociate from the activity by taking such steps as removing their name from written reports or recommendations or asking for a different assignment. Inaction combined with continuing association with those involved in illegal or unethical conduct may be construed as participation or assistance in the illegal or unethical conduct.

Exhibit 1. Global Application of the Code and Standards

Members and candidates who practice in multiple jurisdictions may be subject to varied securities laws and regulations. If applicable law is stricter than the requirements of the Code and Standards, members and candidates must adhere to applicable law; otherwise, they must adhere to the Code and Standards. The following chart provides illustrations involving a member who may be subject to the securities laws and regulations of three different types of countries: Countries with

NSL = no securities laws or regulations
LS = *less* strict securities laws and regulations than the Code and Standards
MS = *more* strict securities laws and regulations than the Code and Standards

Applicable Law	Duties	Explanation
Member resides in NSL country, does business in LS country; LS law applies.	Member must adhere to the Code and Standards.	Because applicable law is less strict than the Code and Standards, the member must adhere to the Code and Standards.
Member resides in NSL country, does business in MS country; MS law applies.	Member must adhere to the law of MS country.	Because applicable law is stricter than the Code and Standards, member must adhere to the more strict applicable law.
Member resides in LS country, does business in NSL country; LS law applies.	Member must adhere to the Code and Standards.	Because applicable law is less strict than the Code and Standards, the member must adhere to the Code and Standards.
Member resides in LS country, does business in MS country; MS law applies.	Member must adhere to the law of MS country.	Because applicable law is stricter than the Code and Standards, the member must adhere to the more strict applicable law.
Member resides in LS country, does business in NSL country; LS law applies, but it states that law of locality where business is conducted governs.	Member must adhere to the Code and Standards.	Because applicable law states that the law of the locality where the business is conducted governs and there is no local law, the member must adhere to the Code and Standards.
Member resides in LS country, does business in MS country; LS law applies, but it states that law of locality where business is conducted governs.	Member must adhere to the law of MS country.	Because applicable law of the locality where the business is conducted governs and local law is stricter than the Code and Standards, the member must adhere to the more strict applicable law.
Member resides in MS country, does business in LS country; MS law applies.	Member must adhere to the law of MS country.	Because applicable law is stricter than the Code and Standards, member must adhere to the more strict applicable law.

Exhibit 1. Global Application of the Code and Standards (continued)		
Applicable Law	**Duties**	**Explanation**
Member resides in MS country, does business in LS country; MS law applies, but it states that law of locality where business is conducted governs.	Member must adhere to the Code and Standards.	Because applicable law states that the law of the locality where the business is conducted governs and local law is less strict than the Code and Standards, the member must adhere to the Code and Standards.
Member resides in MS country, does business in LS country with a client who is a citizen of LS country; MS law applies, but it states that the law of the client's home country governs.	Member must adhere to the Code and Standards.	Because applicable law states that the law of the client's home country governs (which is less strict than the Code and Standards), the member must adhere to the Code and Standards.
Member resides in MS country, does business in LS country with a client who is a citizen of MS country; MS law applies, but it states that the law of the client's home country governs.	Member must adhere to the law of MS country.	Because applicable law states that the law of the client's home country governs and the law of the client's home country is stricter than the Code and Standards, the member must adhere to the more strict applicable law.

Although the Code and Standards do not require that members and candidates report violations to the appropriate governmental or regulatory organizations, such disclosure may be prudent in certain circumstances, and mandated if required by applicable law. Similarly, the Code and Standards do not require that members and candidates report to CFA Institute potential violations of the Code and Standards by fellow members and candidates. However, CFA Institute encourages members, nonmembers, clients, and the investing public to report violations of the Code and Standards by CFA Institute members or CFA candidates by submitting a complaint in writing to the CFA Institute Professional Conduct Program: E-mail pconduct@cfainstitute.org or visit the CFA Institute website at www.cfainstitute.org.

Recommended Procedures for Compliance

Members and Candidates. Suggested methods by which members and candidates can acquire and maintain understanding of applicable laws, rules, and regulations include the following:

- Stay informed. Members and candidates should establish or encourage their employers to establish a procedure by which employees are regularly informed about changes in applicable laws, rules, regulations, and case law. In many instances, the employer's compliance department or legal counsel can provide such information in the form of memorandums distributed to employees in the organization. Also, participation in an internal or external continuing education program is a practical method of staying current.

- Review procedures. Members and candidates should review or encourage their employers to review written compliance procedures on a regular basis in order to ensure that they reflect current law and provide adequate guidance to employees concerning what is permissible conduct under the law and/or the CFA Institute Code and Standards. Recommended compliance procedures for specific items of the CFA Institute Code and Standards are discussed within the guidance associated with each standard.
- Maintain current files. Members and candidates should maintain or encourage their employers to maintain readily accessible current reference copies of applicable statutes, rules, regulations, and important cases.

When in doubt, it is recommended that a member or candidate seek the advice of compliance personnel or legal counsel concerning legal requirements. If the potential violation is committed by a fellow employee, it may also be prudent for the member or candidate to seek the advice of the firm's compliance department or legal counsel.

When dissociating from an activity that violates the Code and Standards, members and candidates should document any violations and urge their firms to attempt to persuade the perpetrator(s) to cease such conduct. It may be necessary for a member or candidate to resign his or her employment to dissociate from the conduct.

Firms. The formality and complexity of compliance procedures for firms depend on the nature and size of the organization and the nature of its investment operations. Members and candidates should encourage their firms to consider the following policies and procedures to support the principles of Standard I:

- Develop and/or adopt a code of ethics. The ethical culture of an organization starts at the top. Members and candidates should encourage their supervisors or management to adopt a code of ethics. Adhering to a code of ethics facilitates solutions when faced with ethical dilemmas and can prevent the need of employees to resort to a "whistle blowing" solution.
- Make available and/or distribute to employees pertinent information that highlights applicable laws and regulations. Information sources may include primary information developed by the relevant government, governmental agencies, regulatory organizations, licensing agencies, and professional associations (e.g., from their websites); law firm memorandums or newsletters; and association memorandums or publications (e.g., *CFA Magazine*).
- Establish written protocols for reporting suspected violations of laws, regulations, and company policies.

Application of the Standard

Example 1. Michael Allen works for a brokerage firm and is responsible for an underwriting of securities. A company official gives Allen information indicating that the financial statements Allen filed with the regulator overstate the issuer's earnings. Allen seeks the advice of the brokerage firm's general counsel, who states that it would be difficult for the regulator to prove that Allen has been involved in any wrongdoing.

> *Comment*: Although it is recommended that members and candidates seek the advice of legal counsel, the reliance on such advice does not absolve a member or candidate from the requirement to comply with the law or regulation. Allen should report this situation to his supervisor, seek an independent legal opinion, and determine whether the regulator should be notified of the error.

Example 2. Lawrence Brown's employer, an investment-banking firm, is the principal underwriter for an issue of convertible debentures by the Courtney Company. Brown discovers that Courtney Company has concealed severe third-quarter losses in its foreign operations. The preliminary prospectus has already been distributed.

> *Comment*: Knowing that the preliminary prospectus is misleading, Brown should report his findings to the appropriate supervisory persons in his firm. If the matter is not remedied and Brown's employer does not dissociate from the underwriting, Brown should sever all his connections with the underwriting. Brown should also seek legal advice to determine whether additional reporting or other action should be taken.

Example 3. Kamisha Washington's firm advertises its past performance record by showing the 10-year return of a composite of its client accounts. However, Washington discovers that the composite omits the performance of accounts that have left the firm during the 10-year period and that this omission has led to an inflated performance figure. Washington is asked to use promotional material that includes the erroneous performance number when soliciting business for the firm.

> *Comment*: Misrepresenting performance is a violation of the Code and Standards. Although she did not calculate the performance herself, Washington would be assisting in violating this standard if she were to use the inflated performance number when soliciting clients. She must dissociate herself from the activity. She can bring the misleading number to the attention of the person responsible for calculating performance, her supervisor, or the compliance department at her firm. If her firm is unwilling to recalculate performance, she must refrain from using the misleading promotional material and should notify the firm of her reasons. If the firm insists that she use the material, she should consider whether her obligation to dissociate from the activity would require her to seek other employment.

Example 4. James Collins is an investment analyst for a major Wall Street brokerage firm. He works in a developing country with a rapidly modernizing economy and a growing capital market. Local securities laws are minimal—in form and content—and include no punitive prohibitions against insider trading.

> *Comment*: Collins should be aware of the risks that a small market and the absence of a fairly regulated flow of information to the market represent to his ability to obtain information and make timely judgments. He should include this factor in formulating his advice to clients. In handling material nonpublic information that accidentally comes into his possession, he must follow Standard II(A).

Example 5. Laura Jameson works for a multinational investment advisor based in the United States. Jameson lives and works as a registered investment advisor in the tiny, but wealthy, island nation of Karramba. Karramba's securities laws state that no investment advisor registered and working in that country can participate in initial public offerings (IPOs) for the advisor's personal account. Jameson, believing that as a U.S. citizen working for a U.S.-based company she need comply only with U.S. law, has ignored this Karrambian law. In addition, Jameson believes that, as a charterholder, as long as she adheres to the Code and Standards requirement that she disclose her participation in any IPO to her employer and clients when such ownership creates a conflict of interest, she is operating on ethical high ground.

> *Comment*: Jameson is in violation of Standard I(A). As a registered investment advisor in Karramba, Jameson is prevented by Karrambian securities law from participating in IPOs regardless of the law of her home country. In addition, because the law of the country where she is working is stricter than the Code and Standards, she must follow the stricter requirements of the local law rather than the requirements of the Code and Standards.

Standard I: Professionalism

(B) Independence and Objectivity

Members and Candidates must use reasonable care and judgment to achieve and maintain independence and objectivity in their professional activities. Members and Candidates must not offer, solicit, or accept any gift, benefit, compensation, or consideration that reasonably could be expected to compromise their own or another's independence and objectivity.

Guidance

Standard I(B) states the responsibility of CFA Institute members and candidates in the CFA Program to maintain independence and objectivity so that their clients will have the benefit of their work and opinions unaffected by any potential conflict of interest or other circumstance adversely affecting their judgment. Every member and candidate should endeavor to avoid situations that could cause or be perceived to cause a loss of independence or objectivity in recommending investments or taking investment action.

External sources may try to influence the investment process by offering analysts and portfolio managers a variety of benefits. Corporations may seek expanded research coverage; issuers and underwriters may wish to promote new securities offerings; brokers may want to increase commission business. Benefits may include gifts, invitations to lavish functions, tickets, favors, job referrals, and so on. One type of benefit is the allocation of shares in oversubscribed IPOs to investment managers for their personal accounts. This practice affords managers the opportunity to make quick profits that may not be available to their clients. Such a practice is prohibited under Standard I(B). Modest gifts and entertainment are acceptable, but special care must be taken by members and candidates to resist subtle and not-so-subtle pressures to act in conflict with the interests of their clients. Best practice dictates that members and candidates must reject any offer of gift or entertainment that could be expected to threaten their independence and objectivity.

Receiving a gift, benefit, or consideration from a client can be distinguished from gifts given by entities seeking to influence a member or candidate to the detriment of other clients. In a client relationship, the client has already entered some type of compensation arrangement with the member, candidate, or his or her firm. A gift from a client could be considered supplementary compensation. The potential for obtaining influence to the detriment of other clients, although present, is not as great as in situations where no compensation arrangement exists. Therefore, members and candidates may accept "bonuses" or gifts from clients but must disclose to their employers such benefits from clients. Disclosure allows the employer of a member or candidate to make an independent determination about the extent to which the gift may affect the member or candidate's independence and objectivity.

Members and candidates may also come under pressure from their own firms to, for example, issue favorable research reports or recommendations for certain companies. The commercial side of a bank may derive substantial revenue from its lending/deposit relationships with a company, and bank managers may be tempted to influence the work of analysts in the investment department. The situation may be aggravated if the head of the company sits on the bank or investment firm's board and attempts to interfere in investment decision making. Members and candidates acting in a sales or marketing capacity must be especially certain of their objectivity in selecting appropriate investments for their clients.

Left unmanaged, pressures that threaten independence place research analysts in a difficult position and may jeopardize their ability to act independently and objectively. One of the ways that research analysts have coped with these pressures in the past is to use subtle and ambiguous language in their recommendations or to temper the tone of their research reports. Such subtleties are lost on some investors who reasonably expect research reports and recommendations to be straightforward and transparent and to communicate clearly an analyst's views based on unbiased analysis and independent judgment.

Members and candidates are personally responsible for maintaining independence and objectivity when preparing research reports, making investment recommendations, and taking investment action on behalf of clients. Recommendations must convey the member or candidate's true opinions, free of bias from internal or external pressures, and be stated in clear and unambiguous language.

Members and candidates also should be aware that some of their professional or social activities within CFA Institute or its member societies may subtly threaten their independence or objectivity. When seeking corporate financial support for conventions, seminars, or even weekly society luncheons, the members or candidates responsible for the activities should evaluate both the actual effect of such solicitations on their independence and whether their objectivity might be perceived to be compromised in the eyes of their clients.

Investment-Banking Relationships. Some sell-side firms may exert pressure on their analysts to issue favorable research on current or prospective investment-banking clients. For many of these firms, income from investment banking has become increasingly important to overall firm profitability because brokerage income has declined as a result of price competition. Consequently, firms offering investment-banking services work hard to develop and maintain relationships with investment-banking clients and prospects. These companies are often covered by the firm's research analysts because companies often select their investment bank based on the reputation of its research analysts, the quality of their work, and their standing in the industry.

Research analysts frequently work closely with their investment-banking colleagues to help evaluate prospective investment-banking clients. Although this practice benefits the firm and enhances market efficiency (e.g., by allowing firms to assess risks more accurately and make better pricing assumptions), it requires firms to carefully balance the conflicts of interest inherent in the collaboration of research and investment banking. Having analysts work with investment bankers is appropriate only when the conflicts are adequately and effectively managed and disclosed. Firm management has a responsibility to provide an environment in which analysts are neither coerced nor enticed into issuing research that does not reflect their true opinions. Firms should require public disclosure of actual conflicts of interest to investors.

Given the symbiotic relationship between research and investment banking, the traditional approach to building "firewalls" between these two functions must be managed to minimize resulting conflicts of interest. It is critical that sell-side firms foster and maintain a corporate culture that fully supports independence and objectivity and protects analysts from undue pressure by their investment-banking colleagues. A key element of an enhanced firewall is separate reporting structures for personnel within the research and investment-banking functions. For example, investment-banking personnel should not have any authority to approve, disapprove, or make changes to research reports or recommendations. Another element should be a compensation arrangement that minimizes the pressures and rewards objectivity and accuracy. Compensation arrangements should not link analyst remuneration directly to investment-banking assignments on which the analyst may participate as a team member. Firms should also regularly review their policies and procedures to determine whether analysts are adequately safeguarded and to improve the transparency of disclosures relating to conflicts of interest. The highest level of transparency is achieved when disclosures are prominent and specific, rather than marginalized and generic.

Public Companies. Analysts can also be pressured to issue favorable reports and recommendations by the companies they follow. Company management often believes that the company's stock is undervalued and may find it difficult to accept critical research reports or ratings downgrades. Management compensation may also be dependent on stock performance. Not every stock is a "buy" and not every research report is favorable – for many reasons, including the cyclical nature of many business activities and market fluctuations. For instance, a "good company" does not always translate into a "good stock" rating if the current stock price is fully valued. In making an investment recommendation, the analyst is responsible for anticipating, interpreting, and assessing a company's prospects and stock-price performance in a factual manner.

Due diligence in financial research and analysis involves gathering information from a wide variety of sources, including company management and investor-relations personnel, suppliers, customers, competitors, and other relevant sources in addition to public disclosure documents, such as proxy statements, annual reports, and other regulatory filings. Research analysts may justifiably fear that companies will limit their ability to conduct thorough research by denying "negative" analysts direct access to company management and/or barring them from conference calls and other communication venues. Retaliatory practices include companies bringing legal action against analysts personally and/or their firms to seek monetary damages for the economic effects of negative reports and recommendations. Although few companies engage in such behavior, the perception that a reprisal is possible is a reasonable concern for analysts. This concern may make it difficult for them to conduct the comprehensive research needed to make objective recommendations. For further information and guidance, members and candidates should refer to the CFA Institute *Best Practice Guidelines Covering Analyst/Corporate Issuer Relations* (www.cfainstitute.org).

Buy-Side Clients. A third source of pressure on sell-side analysts may come from buy-side clients. Institutional clients are traditionally the primary users of sell-side research, either directly or with soft dollar brokerage. Portfolio managers may have significant positions in the security of a company under review. A rating downgrade may adversely affect the portfolio's performance, particularly in the short term, because the sensitivity of stock prices to ratings changes has increased in recent years. A downgrade may also impact the manager's compensation, which is usually tied to portfolio performance. Moreover, portfolio performance is subject to media and public scrutiny, which may affect the manager's professional reputation. Consequently, some portfolio managers may implicitly or explicitly support sell-side ratings inflation.

Portfolio managers have a responsibility to respect and foster the intellectual honesty of sell-side research. Therefore, it is improper for portfolio managers to threaten or engage in retaliatory practices, such as reporting sell-side analysts to the covered company to instigate negative corporate reactions. Although most portfolio managers do not engage in such practices, the perception by the research analyst that a reprisal is possible may cause concern, making it difficult to maintain independence and objectivity.

Issuer-Paid Research. In light of the recent reduction of sell-side research coverage, many companies, seeking to increase visibility both in the financial markets and with potential investors, hire analysts to produce research reports analyzing their companies. These reports bridge the gap created by the lack of coverage and can be an effective method of communicating with investors.

Issuer-paid research, however, is fraught with potential conflicts. Depending on how the research is written and distributed, investors can be misled into believing that research appears to be from an independent source when, in reality, it has been paid for by the subject company.

It is critical that research analysts adhere to strict standards of conduct that govern how the research is to be conducted and what disclosures must be made in the report. Analysts must engage in thorough, independent, and unbiased analysis and must fully disclose potential conflicts, including the nature of their compensation. Otherwise, analysts risk misleading investors by becoming an extension of an issuer's public relations department while appearing to produce "independent" analysis.

Investors need clear, credible, and thorough information about companies and research based on independent thought. At a minimum, research should include a thorough analysis of the company's financial statements based on publicly disclosed information, benchmarking within a peer group, and industry analysis. Analysts must exercise diligence, independence, and thoroughness in conducting their research in an objective manner. Analysts must distinguish between fact and opinion in their reports. Conclusions must have a reasonable and adequate basis, and must be supported by appropriate research.

Analysts must also strictly limit the type of compensation that they accept for conducting research. Otherwise, the content and conclusions of the reports could reasonably be expected to be determined or affected by compensation from the sponsoring companies. This compensation can be as direct, such as payment based on the conclusions of the report or more indirect, such as stock warrants or other equity instruments that could increase in value based on positive coverage in the report. In those instances, analysts would have an incentive to avoid negative information or conclusions that would diminish their potential compensation. Best practice is for analysts to accept only a flat fee for their work prior to writing the report, without regard to their conclusions or the report's recommendations.

Recommended Procedures for Compliance

Members and candidates should follow certain practices and should encourage their firms to establish certain procedures to avoid violations of Standard I(B):

- Protect integrity of opinions. Members, candidates, and their firms should establish policies stating that every research report on issues by a corporate client reflects the unbiased opinion of the analyst. Firms should also design compensation systems that protect the integrity of the investment decision process by maintaining the independence and objectivity of analysts.
- Create a restricted list. If the firm is unwilling to permit dissemination of adverse opinions about a corporate client, members and candidates should encourage the firm to remove the controversial company from the research universe and put it on a restricted list so that the firm disseminates only factual information about the company.

- Restrict special cost arrangements. When attending meetings at an issuer's headquarters, members or candidates should pay for commercial transportation and hotel charges. No corporate issuer should reimburse members or candidates for air transportation. Members and candidates should encourage issuers to limit the use of corporate aircraft to situations in which commercial transportation is not available or in which efficient movement could not otherwise be arranged. Members and candidates should take particular care that when frequent meetings are held between an individual issuer and an individual member or candidate, the issuer should not always host the member or candidate.
- Limit gifts. Members and candidates must limit the acceptance of gratuities and/or gifts to token items. Standard I(B) does not preclude customary, ordinary, business-related entertainment so long as its purpose is not to influence or reward members or candidates.
- Restrict investments. Members and candidates should restrict (or encourage their investment firms to restrict) employee purchases of equity or equity-related IPOs. Strict limits should be imposed on investment personnel acquiring securities in private placements.
- Review procedures. Members and candidates should implement (or encourage their firms to implement) effective supervisory and review procedures to ensure that analysts and portfolio managers comply with policies relating to their personal investment activities.
- Firms should establish a formal written policy on the independence and objectivity of research and implement reporting structures and review procedures to ensure that research analysts do not report to and are not supervised or controlled by any department of the firm that could compromise the independence of the analyst. More detailed recommendations related to a firm's policies regarding research objectivity are set forth in the CFA Institute Research Objectivity Standards. (www.cfainstitute.org)

Application of the Standard

Example 1. Steven Taylor, a mining analyst with Bronson Brokers, is invited by Precision Metals to join a group of his peers in a tour of mining facilities in several western U.S. states. The company arranges for chartered group flights from site to site and for accommodations in Spartan Motels, the only chain with accommodations near the mines, for three nights. Taylor allows Precision Metals to pick up his tab, as do the other analysts, with one exception–John Adams, an employee of a large trust company who insists on following his company's policy and paying for his hotel room himself.

Comment: The policy of Adams's company complies closely with Standard I(B) by avoiding even the appearance of a conflict of interest, but Taylor and the other analysts were not necessarily violating Standard I(B). In general, when allowing companies to pay for travel and/or accommodations under these circumstances, members and candidates must use their judgment–keeping in mind that such arrangements must not impinge on a member or candidate's independence and objectivity. In this example, the trip was strictly for business and Taylor was not accepting irrelevant or lavish hospitality. The itinerary required chartered flights, for which analysts were not expected to pay. The accommodations were modest. These arrangements are not unusual and did not violate Standard I(B) so long as Taylor's independence and objectivity were not compromised. In the final analysis, members and candidates should consider both whether they can remain objective and whether their integrity might be perceived by their clients to have been compromised.

Example 2. Susan Dillon, an analyst in the corporate finance department of an investment services firm, is making a presentation to a potential new business client that includes the promise that her firm will provide full research coverage of the potential client.

Comment: Dillon may agree to provide research coverage, but she must not commit her firm's research department to providing a favorable recommendation. The firm's recommendation (favorable, neutral, or unfavorable) must be based on an independent and objective investigation and analysis of the company and its securities.

Example 3. Walter Fritz is an equity analyst with Hilton Brokerage who covers the mining industry. He has concluded that the stock of Metals & Mining is overpriced at its current level, but he is concerned that a negative research report will hurt the good relationship between Metals & Mining and the investment-banking division of his firm. In fact, a senior manager of Hilton Brokerage has just sent him a copy of a proposal his firm has made to Metals & Mining to underwrite a debt offering. Fritz needs to produce a report right away and is concerned about issuing a less-than-favorable rating.

Comment: Fritz's analysis of Metals & Mining must be objective and based solely on consideration of company fundamentals. Any pressure from other divisions of his firm is inappropriate. This conflict could have been eliminated if, in anticipation of the offering, Hilton Brokerage had placed Metals & Mining on a restricted list for its sales force.

Example 4. As support for the sales effort of her corporate bond department, Lindsey Warner offers credit guidance to purchasers of fixed-income securities. Her compensation is closely linked to the performance of the corporate bond department. Near the quarter's end, Warner's firm has a large inventory position in the bonds of Milton, Ltd., and has been unable to sell the bonds because of Milton's recent announcement of an operating problem. Salespeople have asked her to contact large clients to push the bonds.

> *Comment:* Unethical sales practices create significant potential violations of the Code and Standards. Warner's opinion of the Milton bonds must not be affected by internal pressure or compensation. In this case, Warner must refuse to push the Milton bonds unless she is able to justify that the market price has already adjusted for the operating problem.

Example 5. Jill Jorund is a securities analyst following airline stocks and a rising star at her firm. Her boss has been carrying a "buy" recommendation on International Airlines and asks Jorund to take over coverage of that airline. He tells Jorund that under no circumstances should the prevailing "buy" recommendation be changed.

> *Comment:* Jorund must be independent and objective in her analysis of International Airlines. If she believes that her boss's instructions have compromised her, she has two options: Tell her boss that she cannot cover the company under these constraints or pick up coverage of the company, reach her own independent conclusions, and if they conflict with her boss's opinion, share the conclusions with her boss or other supervisors in the firm so that they can make appropriate recommendations. Jorund must only issue recommendations that reflect only her independent and objective opinion.

Example 6. Edward Grant directs a large amount of his commission business to a New York-based brokerage house. In appreciation for all the business, the brokerage house gives Grant two tickets to the World Cup in South Africa, two nights at a nearby resort, several meals, and transportation via limousine to the game. Grant fails to disclose receiving this package to his supervisor.

> *Comment:* Grant has violated Standard I(B) because accepting these substantial gifts may impede his independence and objectivity. Every member and candidate should endeavor to avoid situations that might cause or be perceived to cause a loss of independence or objectivity in recommending investments or taking investment action. By accepting the trip, Grant has opened himself up to the accusation that he may give the broker favored treatment in return.

Example 7. Theresa Green manages the portfolio of Ian Knowlden, a client of Tisbury Investments. Green achieves an annual return for Knowlden that is consistently better than that of the benchmark she and the client previously agreed to. As a reward, Knowlden offers Green two tickets to Wimbledon and the use of Knowlden's flat in London for a week. Green discloses this gift to her supervisor at Tisbury.

Comment: Green is in compliance with Standard I(B) because she disclosed the gift from one of her clients. Members and candidates may accept bonuses or gifts from clients so long as they disclose them to their employers, because gifts in a client relationship are deemed less likely to affect a member or candidate's objectivity and independence than gifts in other situations. Disclosure is required, however, so that supervisors can monitor such situations to guard against employees favoring a gift-giving client to the detriment of other fee-paying clients (such as by allocating a greater proportion of IPO stock to the gift-giving client's portfolio).

Example 8. Tom Wayne is the investment manager of the Franklin City Employees Pension Plan. He recently completed a successful search for a firm to manage the foreign equity allocation of the plan's diversified portfolio. He followed the plan's standard procedure of seeking presentations from a number of qualified firms and recommended that his board select Penguin Advisors because of its experience, well-defined investment strategy, and performance record, which was compiled and verified in accordance with the CFA Institute Global Investment Performance Standards. Following the plan selection of Penguin, a reporter from the Franklin City Record called to ask if there was any connection between this action and the fact that Penguin was one of the sponsors of an "investment fact-finding trip to Asia" that Wayne made earlier in the year. The trip was one of several conducted by the Pension Investment Academy, which had arranged the itinerary of meetings with economic, government, and corporate officials in major cities in several Asian countries. The Pension Investment Academy obtains support for the cost of these trips from a number of investment managers, including Penguin Advisors; the Academy then pays the travel expenses of the various pension plan managers on the trip and provides all meals and accommodations. The president of Penguin Advisors was one of the travelers on the trip.

> *Comment*: Although Wayne can probably put to good use the knowledge he gained from the trip in selecting portfolio managers and in other areas of managing the pension plan, his recommendation of Penguin Advisors may be tainted by the possible conflict incurred when he participated in a trip paid partly for by Penguin Advisors and when he was in the daily company of the president of Penguin Advisors. To avoid violating Standard I(B), Wayne's basic expenses for travel and accommodations should have been paid by his employer or the pension plan; contact with the president of Penguin Advisors should have been limited to informational or educational events only; and the trip, the organizer, and the sponsor should have been made a matter of public record. Even if his actions were not in violation of Standard I(B), Wayne should have been sensitive to the public perception of the trip when reported in the newspaper and the extent to which the subjective elements of his decision might have been affected by the familiarity that the daily contact of such a trip would encourage. This advantage would probably not be shared by competing firms.

Example 9. Javier Herrero recently left his job as a research analyst for a large investment advisor. While looking for a new position, he is hired by an investor-relations firm to write a research report on one of its clients, a small educational software company. The investor-relations firm hopes to generate investor interest in the technology company. The firm will pay Herrero a flat fee plus a bonus if any new investors buy stock in the company as a result of Herrero's report.

> *Comment:* If Herrero accepts this payment arrangement, he will be in violation of Standard I(B) because the compensation can reasonably be expected to compromise his independence and objectivity. Herrero will receive a bonus for attracting investors, which is an overwhelming incentive to draft a positive report regardless of the facts and to ignore or play down any negative information about the company. Herrero should accept for his work only a flat fee that is not tied to the conclusions or recommendations of the report. Issuer-paid research that is objective and unbiased can be done under the right circumstances so long as the analyst takes steps to maintain his or her objectivity and includes in the report proper disclosures regarding potential conflicts of interest.

Standard I: Professionalism

(C) Misrepresentation

Members and Candidates must not knowingly make any misrepresentations relating to investment analysis, recommendations, actions, or other professional activities.

Guidance

Trust is the foundation of the investment profession. Investors must be able to rely on the statements and information provided to them by those with whom investors trust their financial well being. Investment professionals who make false or misleading statements not only harm investors but also reduce the level of investor confidence in the investment profession and threaten the integrity of capital markets as a whole.

A misrepresentation is any untrue statement or omission of a fact or any statement that is otherwise false or misleading. A member or candidate must not knowingly misrepresent or give a false impression in oral representations, advertising (whether in the press or through brochures), electronic communications, or written materials (whether publicly disseminated or not). In this context, "knowingly" means that a member or candidate either knows or should have known that the misrepresentation was being made.

Written materials for a general audience include, but are not limited to, research reports, market letters, newspaper columns, and books. Electronic communications include, but are not limited to, Internet communications, Web pages, chat rooms, and e-mail.

Members and candidates must not misrepresent any aspect of their practice, including (but not limited to) their qualifications or credentials, the qualifications or services provided by their firm, their performance record or the record of their firm, or the characteristics of an investment. Any misrepresentation made by the member or candidate relating to the member or candidate's professional activities is a breach of this standard.

Standard I(C) prohibits members and candidates from guaranteeing clients specific return on investments that are inherently volatile. ("I can guarantee that you will earn 8 percent on equities this year," or "I can guarantee that you will not lose money on this investment"). For the most part, the majority of investments contain some element of risk that makes their return inherently unpredictable. In those situations, guaranteeing either a particular rate of return or a guaranteed preservation of investment capital is misleading to investors. Standard I(C) does not prohibit members and candidates from providing clients with information on investment products that have guarantees built in to the structure of the product itself or for which an institution has agreed to cover any losses.

Standard I(C) also prohibits plagiarism in the preparation of material for distribution to employers, associates, clients, prospects, or the general public. Plagiarism is defined as copying or using in substantially the same form materials prepared by others without acknowledging the source of the material or identifying the author and publisher of such material. Members and candidates must not copy, or represent as their own, original ideas or material without permission and must acknowledge and identify the source of ideas or material that is not their own.

The investment profession uses a myriad of financial, economic, and statistical data in the investment decision-making process. Through various publications and presentations, the investment professional is constantly exposed to the work of others and to the temptation to use that work without proper acknowledgment.

Misrepresentation through plagiarism in investment management can take various forms. The simplest and most flagrant example is to take a research report or study done by another firm or person, change the names, and release the material as one's own original analysis. This action is a clear violation of Standard I(C). Other practices include (1) using excerpts from articles or reports prepared by others either verbatim or with only slight changes in wording without acknowledgment, (2) citing specific quotations supposedly attributable to "leading analysts" and "investment experts" without specific reference, (3) presenting statistical estimates of forecasts prepared by others with the source identified but without qualifying statements or caveats that may have been used, (4) using charts and graphs without stating their sources, and (5) copying proprietary computerized spreadsheets or algorithms without seeking the cooperation or authorization of their creators.

In the case of distributing third-party, outsourced research, members and candidates can use and distribute these reports so long as they do not represent themselves as the author of the report. The member or candidate may add value to the client by sifting through research and repackaging it for clients. The client should fully understand that he or she is paying for the ability of the member or candidate to find the best research from a wide variety of sources. However, members and candidates must not misrepresent their abilities, the extent of their expertise, or the extent of their work in a way that would mislead their clients or prospective clients. Members and candidates should consider disclosing whether the research being presented to clients comes from an outside source, from either within or outside the members or candidate's firm. Clients should know who has the expertise behind the report or if the work is being done by the analyst, other members of the firm, or an outside party.

The standard also applies to plagiarism in oral communications, such as through group meetings; visits with associates, clients, and customers; use of audio/video media (which is rapidly increasing); and telecommunications, such as through electronic data transfer and the outright copying of electronic media.

One of the most egregious practices in violation of this standard is the preparation of research reports based on multiple sources of information without acknowledging the sources. Such information would include, for example, ideas, statistical compilations, and forecasts combined to give the appearance of original work. Although there is no monopoly on ideas, members and candidates must give credit when it is clearly due. Analysts should not use undocumented forecasts, earnings projections, asset values, and so on. Sources must be revealed to bring the responsibility directly back to the author of the report or the firm involved.

Recommended Procedures for Compliance

Members and candidates can prevent unintentional misrepresentations of the qualifications or services they or their firms provide if each member and candidate understands the limit of the firm or individual's capabilities and the need to be accurate and complete in presentations. Firms can provide guidance for employees who make written or oral presentations to clients or potential clients by providing a written list of the firm's available services and a description of the firm's qualifications. This list should suggest ways of describing the firm's services, qualifications, and compensation that are both accurate and suitable for client or customer presentations. Firms can also help prevent misrepresentation by specifically designating which employees are authorized to speak on behalf of the firm. Whether or not the firm provides guidance, members and candidates should make certain they understand the services the firm can perform and its qualifications.

In addition, in order to ensure accurate presentations to clients, each member and candidate should prepare a summary of his or her own qualifications and experience as well as a list of the services the member or candidate is capable of performing. Firms can assist member and candidate compliance by periodically reviewing employee correspondence and documents that contain representations of individual or firm qualifications.

Members and candidates who publish Web pages should regularly monitor materials posted to the site to ensure the site maintains current information. Members and candidates should also ensure that all reasonable precautions have been taken to protect the site's integrity, confidentiality, and security and that the site does not misrepresent any information and provides full disclosure.

To avoid plagiarism in preparing research reports or conclusions of analysis, members and candidates should take the following steps:

- Maintain copies. Keep copies of all research reports, articles containing research ideas, material with new statistical methodology, and other materials that were relied on in preparing the research report.

- Attribute quotations. Attribute to their sources any direct quotations, including projections, tables, statistics, model/product ideas, and new methodologies prepared by persons other than recognized financial and statistical reporting services or similar sources.
- Attribute summaries. Attribute to their sources paraphrases or summaries of material prepared by others. For example, to support his analysis of Brown's competitive position, the author of a research report on Brown Company may summarize another analyst's report of Brown's chief competitor, but the author of the Brown report must acknowledge in his own report his reliance on the other analyst's report.

Application of the Standard

Example 1. Allison Rogers is a partner in the firm of Rogers and Black, a small firm offering investment advisory services. She assures a prospective client who has just inherited $1 million that "we can perform all the financial and investment services you need." Rogers and Black is well equipped to provide investment advice but, in fact, cannot provide asset allocation assistance or a full array of financial and investment services.

Comment: Rogers has violated Standard I(C) by orally misrepresenting the services her firm can perform for the prospective client. She must limit herself to describing the range of investment advisory services Rogers and Black can provide and offer to help the client obtain elsewhere the financial and investment services that her firm cannot provide.

Example 2. Anthony McGuire is an issuer-paid analyst hired by publicly traded companies to electronically promote their stocks. McGuire creates a website that promotes his research efforts as a seemingly independent analyst. McGuire posts a profile and a strong buy recommendation for each company on the website indicating that the stock is expected to increase in value. He does not disclose the contractual relationships with the companies he covers on his website, in the research reports he issues, or in the statements he makes about the companies on Internet chat rooms.

Comment: McGuire has violated Standard I(C) because the Internet site and e-mails are misleading to potential investors. Even if the recommendations are valid and supported with thorough research, his omissions regarding the true relationship between himself and the companies he covers constitute a misrepresentation. McGuire has also violated Standard VI(C) by not disclosing the existence of an arrangement with the companies through which he receives compensation in exchange for his services.

Example 3. Hijan Yao is responsible for the creation and distribution of the marketing material for his firm. Yao creates and distributes a performance presentation for the firm's Asian equity composite that complies with GIPS and states that the composite has 350 billion yen in assets. In fact, the composite has only 35 billion yen in assets, and the higher figure on the presentation is a result of a typographical error. Nevertheless, the erroneous material is distributed to a number of clients before Yao catches the mistake.

> *Comment:* Once the error is discovered, Yao must take steps to cease distribution of the incorrect material and correct the error by informing those who have received the erroneous information. However, because Yao did not knowingly make the misrepresentation, he did not violate the Code and Standards.

Example 4. Syed Muhammad is the president of an investment management firm. The promotional material for the firm, created by the firm's marketing department, incorrectly claims that Muhammad has an advanced degree in finance from a prestigious business school in addition to the CFA designation. Although Muhammad attended the school for a short period of time, he did not receive a degree. Over the years, Muhammad and others in the firm have distributed this material to numerous prospective clients and consultants.

> *Comment:* Even though Muhammad may not have been directly responsible for the misrepresentation about his credentials contained in the firm's promotional material, he used this material numerous times over an extended period and should have known of the misrepresentation. Thus, Muhammad has violated Standard I(C).

Example 5. Cindy Grant, a research analyst for a Canadian brokerage firm, has specialized in the Canadian mining industry for the past 10 years. She recently read an extensive research report on Jefferson Mining, Ltd., by Jeremy Barton, another analyst. Barton provided extensive statistics on the mineral reserves, production capacity, selling rates, and marketing factors affecting Jefferson's operations. He also noted that initial drilling results on a new ore body, which had not been made public, might show the existence of mineral zones that could increase the life of Jefferson's main mines, but Barton cited no specific data as to the initial drilling results. Grant called an officer of Jefferson, who gave her the initial drilling results over the telephone. The data indicated that the expected life of the main mines would be tripled. Grant added these statistics to Barton's report and circulated it as her own report within her firm.

> *Comment:* Grant plagiarized Barton's report by reproducing large parts of it in her own report without acknowledgment.

Example 6. When Ricki Marks sells mortgage-backed derivatives called interest-only strips (IOs) to her public pension plan clients, she describes them as "guaranteed by the U.S. government." Purchasers of the IOs, however, are entitled only to the interest stream generated by the mortgages not the notional principal itself. The municipality's investment policies and local law require that securities purchased by the public pension plans be guaranteed by the U.S. government. Although the underlying mortgages are guaranteed, neither the investor's investment nor the interest stream on the IOs is guaranteed. When interest rates decline, causing an increase in prepayment of mortgages, the interest payments to the clients decline, and the clients lose a portion of their investment.

> *Comment:* Marks violated Standard I(C) by misrepresenting the terms and character of the investment.

Example 7. Khalouck Abdrabbo, manages the investments of several high-net-worth individuals in the United States who are approaching retirement. Abdrabbo advises that a portion of their investments be moved from equity to certificates of deposit and money-market accounts so the principal will be "guaranteed" up to a certain amount. The interest is not guaranteed.

> *Comment:* While there is risk that the institution offering the certificates of deposits and money-market accounts could go bankrupt, in the United States, these accounts are insured by the U.S. government through the Federal Deposit Insurance Corporation. Therefore, using the term "guaranteed" in this context is not inappropriate as long as the amount is within the government-insured limit. Abdrabbo should explain these facts to the clients.

Example 8. Steve Swanson is a senior analyst in the investment research department of Ballard and Company. Apex Corporation has asked Ballard to assist in acquiring the majority ownership in stock of Campbell Company, a financial consulting firm, and to prepare a report recommending that stockholders of Campbell agree to the acquisition. Another investment firm, Davis and Company, had already prepared a report for Apex analyzing both Apex and Campbell and recommending an exchange ratio. Apex has given the Davis report to Ballard officers, who have passed it on to Swanson, who then reviewed the Davis report along with other available material on Apex and Campbell companies. From his analysis, he concludes that the common stocks of Campbell and Apex represent good value at their current prices; he believes, however, that the Davis report does not consider all the factors a Campbell stockholder would need to know to make a decision. Swanson reports his conclusions to the partner in charge, who tells him to "use the Davis report, change a few words, sign your name, and get it out."

> *Comment:* If Swanson does as requested, he will violate Standard I(C). He could refer to those portions of the Davis report that he agrees with if he identifies Davis as the source; he could then add his own analysis and conclusions to the report before signing and distributing it.

Example 9. Claude Browning, a quantitative analyst for Double Alpha, Inc., returns in great excitement from a seminar. In that seminar, Jack Jorrely, a well-publicized quantitative analyst at a national brokerage firm, discussed one of his new models in great detail, and Browning is intrigued by the new concepts. He proceeds to test this model, making some minor mechanical changes but retaining the concept, until he produces some very positive results. Browning quickly announces to his supervisors at Double Alpha that he has discovered a new model and that clients and prospective clients alike should be informed of this positive finding as ongoing proof of Double Alpha's continuing innovation and ability to add value.

> *Comment:* Although Browning tested Jorrely's model on his own and even slightly modified it, he must still acknowledge the original source of the idea. Browning can certainly take credit for the final, practical results; he can also support his conclusions with his own test. The credit for the innovative thinking, however, must be awarded to Jorrely.

Example 10. Fernando Zubia would like to include in his firm's marketing materials plain-language descriptions of various concepts, such as the price-to-earnings multiple and why standard deviation is used as a measure of risk, that are taken from other sources without reference to the original author. Is this a violation of Standard I(C)?

> *Comment:* Copying verbatim any material without acknowledgement, including plain-language descriptions of the price-to-earnings multiple and standard deviation, violates Standard I(C). Even though these are general concepts, best practice would be for Zubia to describe them in his own words or cite the source from which the descriptions are quoted. Members and candidates responsible for creating marketing materials and those who knowingly use plagiarized materials could potentially be sanctioned if the matter was brought to the attention of the CFA Institute Professional Conduct Program.

Example 11. Through a mainstream media outlet, Erika Schneider learns about a study that she would like to cite in her research. Should she cite both the mainstream intermediary source as well as the author of the study itself when using that information?

> *Comment:* In all instances, it is necessary to cite the actual source of the information. Best practice would be to obtain the information directly from the author and review it before citing it in a report. In that instance, Schneider would not need to report how she found out about the information. For example, suppose Schneider reads in the *Financial Times* about a study issued by CFA Institute; best practice for Schneider would be to obtain a copy of the study from CFA Institute, review it, and then cite it in her report. If she does not use any interpretation from the *Financial Times* and it is not adding value to the report itself, the newspaper is merely a conduit to the original

information she wants to use in the report and it need not be cited. If she does not obtain the report and review the information, Schneider runs the risk of relying on second-hand information that may misstate the source. If, for example, the *Financial Times* erroneously reported the information from the original CFA Institute study and Schneider copied that erroneous information without acknowledging CFA Institute, she would open herself to complaint. Best practice would be either to obtain the complete study from its original author and cite only that author or to use the information provided by the intermediary and cite both sources.

Example 12. Gary Ostrowski runs a small, two-person investment management firm. Ostrowski's firm subscribes to a service from a large investment research firm that provides research reports that can be repackaged as in-house research from smaller firms. Ostrowski's firm distributes these reports to clients as its own work.

Comment: Ostrowski can rely on third-party research that has a reasonable and adequate basis, but he cannot imply that he is the author of the report. Otherwise, Ostrowski would misrepresent the extent of his work in a way that would mislead the firm's clients or prospective clients.

Standard I: Professionalism

(D) Misconduct

Members and Candidates must not engage in any professional conduct involving dishonesty, fraud, or deceit or commit any act that reflects adversely on their professional reputation, integrity, or competence.

Guidance

Whereas Standard I(A) addresses the obligation of members and candidates to comply with applicable law that governs their professional activities, Standard I(D) addresses conduct that reflects poorly on the professional integrity, good reputation, or competence of members and candidates. Although CFA Institute discourages any sort of unethical behavior by members and candidates, the Code and Standards are aimed at conduct related to a member or candidate's professional life. Any act that involves lying, cheating, stealing, or other dishonest conduct that reflects adversely on a member or candidate's professional activities would violate this standard.

Conduct that damages trustworthiness or competence can include behavior that may not be illegal but could negatively affect a member or candidate's ability to perform his or her responsibilities. For example, abusing alcohol during business hours could constitute a violation of this standard because it could have a detrimental effect on the member or candidate's ability to fulfill his or her professional responsibilities. Personal bankruptcy may not reflect on the integrity or trustworthiness of the person declaring bankruptcy, but if the circumstances of the bankruptcy involve fraudulent or deceitful business conduct, it may be a violation of this standard.

Individuals may attempt to abuse the CFA Institute Professional Conduct Program by actively seeking CFA Institute enforcement of the Code and Standards, and Standard I(D) in particular, as a method to settle personal, political, or other disputes unrelated to professional ethics. CFA Institute is aware of this issue, and appropriate disciplinary policies, procedures, and enforcement mechanisms are in place to address misuse of the Code and Standards and the Professional Conduct Program in this way.

Recommended Procedures for Compliance

To prevent general misconduct, members and candidates should encourage their firms to adopt the following policies and procedures to support the principles of Standard I(D):

- Develop and/or adopt a code of ethics to which every employee must subscribe and make clear that any personal behavior that reflects poorly on the individual involved, the institution as a whole, or the investment industry will not be tolerated.
- Disseminate to all employees a list of potential violations and associated disciplinary sanctions, up to and including dismissal from the firm.
- Check references of potential employees to ensure that they are of good character and not ineligible to work in the investment industry because of past infractions of the law.

Application of the Standard

Example 1. Simon Sasserman is a trust investment officer at a bank in a small affluent town. He enjoys lunching every day with friends at the country club, where his clients have observed him having numerous drinks. Back at work after lunch, he clearly is intoxicated while making investment decisions. His colleagues make a point of handling any business with Sasserman in the morning because they distrust his judgment after lunch.

> *Comment:* Sasserman's excessive drinking at lunch and subsequent intoxication at work constitute a violation of Standard I(D) because this conduct has raised questions about his professionalism and competence. His behavior thus reflects poorly on him, his employer, and the investment industry.

Example 2. Howard Hoffman, a security analyst at ATZ Brothers, Inc., a large brokerage house, submits reimbursement forms over a two-year period to ATZ's self-funded health insurance program for more than two dozen bills, most of which have been altered to increase the amount due. An investigation by the firm's director of employee benefits uncovers the conduct. ATZ subsequently terminates Hoffman's employment and notifies CFA Institute.

> *Comment:* Hoffman violated Standard I(D) because he engaged in intentional conduct involving fraud and deceit in the workplace that adversely reflected on his honesty.

Example 3. Jody Brink, an analyst covering the automotive industry, volunteers much of her spare time to local charities. The board of one of the charitable institutions decides to buy five new vans to deliver hot lunches to low-income elderly people. Brink offers to donate her time to handle purchasing agreements. To pay a long-standing debt to a friend who operates an automobile dealership–and to compensate herself for her trouble–she agrees to a price 20 percent higher than normal and splits the surcharge with her friend. The director of the charity ultimately discovers the scheme and tells Brink that her services, donated or otherwise, are no longer required.

> *Comment:* Brink engaged in conduct involving dishonesty, fraud, and misrepresentation and has violated Standard I(D).

Example 4. Carmen Garcia manages a mutual fund dedicated to socially responsible investing. She is also an environmental activist. As the result of her participation at nonviolent protests, Garcia has been arrested on numerous occasions for trespassing on the property of a large petrochemical plant that is accused of damaging the environment.

> *Comment:* Generally, Standard I(D) is not meant to cover legal transgressions resulting from acts of civil disobedience in support of personal beliefs because such conduct does not reflect poorly on the member or candidate's professional reputation, integrity, or competence.

Standard II: Integrity of Capital Markets

(A) Material Nonpublic Information

Members and Candidates who possess material nonpublic information that could affect the value of an investment must not act or cause others to act on the information.

Guidance

Trading on material nonpublic information erodes confidence in capital markets, institutions, and investment professionals by supporting the idea that those with inside information and special access can take unfair advantage of the general investing public. Although trading on inside information may lead to short-term profits, in the long run, individuals and the profession as a whole will suffer as investors avoid capital markets perceived to be "rigged" in favor of the knowledgeable insider. Standard II(A) promotes and maintains a high level of confidence in market integrity, which is one of the foundations of the investment profession.

Information is "material" if its disclosure would likely have an impact on the price of a security or if reasonable investors would want to know the information before making an investment decision. In other words, information is material if it would significantly alter the total mix of information currently available regarding a security such that the price of the security would be affected.

The specificity of the information, the extent of its difference from public information, its nature, and its reliability are key factors in determining whether a particular piece of information fits the definition of material. For example, material information may include, but is not limited to, information on the following:

- earnings;
- mergers, acquisitions, tender offers, or joint ventures;
- changes in assets;
- innovative products, processes, or discoveries;
- new licenses, patents, registered trademarks, or regulatory approval/rejection of a product;
- developments regarding customers or suppliers (e.g., the acquisition or loss of a contract);
- changes in management;
- change in auditor notification or the fact that the issuer may no longer rely on an auditor's report or qualified opinion;

- events regarding the issuer's securities (e.g., defaults on senior securities, calls of securities for redemption, repurchase plans, stock splits, changes in dividends, changes to the rights of security holders, public or private sales of additional securities, and changes in credit ratings);
- bankruptcies;
- significant legal disputes;
- government reports of economic trends (employment, housing starts, currency information, etc.);
- orders for large trades before they are executed.

In addition to the substance and specificity of the information, the source or relative reliability of the information also determines materiality. The less reliable a source, the less likely the information provided would be considered material. For example, factual information from a corporate insider regarding a significant new contract for a company would likely be material, while an assumption based on speculation by a competitor about the same contract might be less reliable and, therefore, not material.

Also, the more ambiguous the effect on price, the less material the information becomes. If it is unclear whether the information will affect the price of a security and to what extent, information may not be considered material. The passage of time may also render information that was once important immaterial.

Information is "nonpublic" until it has been disseminated or is available to the marketplace in general (as opposed to a select group of investors). Dissemination can be defined as "made known to." For example, a company report of profits that is posted on the Internet and distributed widely through a press release or accompanied by a filing has been effectively disseminated to the marketplace. Members and candidates must have a reasonable expectation that people have received the information before it can be considered public. It is not necessary, however, to wait for the slowest method of delivery. Once the information is disseminated to the market, it is public information that is no longer covered by this standard.

Members and candidates must be particularly aware of information that is selectively disclosed by corporations to a small group of investors, analysts, or other market participants. Information that is made available to analysts remains nonpublic until it is made available to investors in general. Corporations that disclose information on a limited basis create the potential for insider-trading violations.

Issues of selective disclosure often arise when a corporate insider provides material information to analysts in a briefing or conference call before that information is released to the public. Analysts must be aware that a disclosure made to a room full of analysts does not necessarily make the disclosed information "public." Analysts should also be alert to the possibility that they are selectively receiving material nonpublic information when a company provides them with guidance or interpretation of such publicly available information as financial statements or regulatory filings.

Mosaic Theory. A financial analyst gathers and interprets large quantities of information from many sources. The analyst may use significant conclusions derived from the analysis of public and nonmaterial nonpublic information as the basis for investment recommendations and decisions even if those conclusions would have been material inside information had they been communicated directly to the analyst by a company. Under the "mosaic theory," financial analysts are free to act on this collection, or mosaic, of information without risking violation.

The practice of financial analysis depends on the free flow of information. For the fair and efficient operation of the capital markets, analysts and investors must have the greatest amount of information possible to facilitate well-informed investment decisions about how and where to invest capital. Accurate, timely, and intelligible communication are essential if analysts and investors are to obtain the data needed to make informed decisions about how and where to invest capital. These disclosures must go beyond the information mandated by the reporting requirements of the securities laws and should include specific business information about items used to guide a company's future growth, such as new products, capital projects, and the competitive environment. Analysts seek and use such information to compare and contrast investment alternatives.

Much of the information used by analysts comes directly from companies. Analysts often receive such information through contacts with corporate insiders, especially investor relations and finance officers. Information may be disseminated in the form of press releases, through oral presentations by company executives in analysts' meetings or conference calls, or during analysts' visits to company premises. In seeking to develop the most accurate and complete picture of a company, analysts should also reach beyond contacts with companies themselves and collect information from other sources, such as customers, contractors, suppliers, and companies' competitors.

Analysts are in the business of formulating opinions and insights—not obvious to the general investing public—concerning the attractiveness of particular securities. In the course of their work, analysts actively seek out corporate information not generally known to the market for the express purpose of analyzing that information, forming an opinion on its significance, and informing their clients who can be expected to trade on the basis of the recommendation. Analysts' initiatives to discover and analyze information and communicate their findings to their clients significantly enhance market efficiency, thus benefiting all investors (see, *Dirks v. Securities and Exchange Commission*).

Accordingly, violations of Standard II(A) will *not* result when a perceptive analyst reaches a conclusion about a corporate action or event through an analysis of public information and items of nonmaterial nonpublic information. Investment professionals should note, however, that although analysts are free to use mosaic information in their research reports, they should save and document all their research [see Standard V(C)]. Evidence of the analyst's knowledge of public and nonmaterial nonpublic information about a corporation strengthens the assertion that the analyst reached his or her conclusions solely through appropriate methods rather than through the use of material nonpublic information.

When a particularly well-known or respected analyst issues a report or makes changes to his or her recommendation, that information alone could have an effect on the market and, thus, could be considered material. Theoretically, under this standard, such a report would have to be made public before it was distributed to clients. However, the analyst is not a company insider and does not have access to inside information. Presumably, the analyst created the report with information available to the public (mosaic theory) using his or her expertise to interpret the information. The analyst's hard work, paid for by the client, generated the conclusions. Simply because the public in general would find the conclusions material does not require that the analyst make his or her work public. Investors who are not clients of the analyst can either do the work themselves or become a client of the analyst if they want access to the analyst's expertise.

Recommended Procedures for Compliance

If a member or candidate determines that information is material, the member or candidate should make reasonable efforts to achieve public dissemination of the information. This effort usually entails encouraging the issuer company to make the information public. If public dissemination is not possible, the member or candidate must communicate the information only to the designated supervisory and compliance personnel within the member or candidate's firm and must not take investment action on the basis of the information. Moreover, members and candidates must not knowingly engage in any conduct that may induce company insiders to privately disclose material nonpublic information.

Members and candidates should encourage their firms to adopt compliance procedures to prevent the misuse of material nonpublic information. Particularly important is improving compliance in such areas as the review of employee and proprietary trading, documentation of firm procedures, and the supervision of interdepartmental communications in multi-service firms. Compliance procedures should suit the particular characteristics of a firm, including its size and the nature of its business.

Members and candidates should encourage their firms to develop and follow disclosure policies designed to ensure that information is disseminated to the marketplace in an equitable manner. For example, analysts from small firms should receive the same information and attention from a company as analysts from large firms receive. Similarly, companies should not provide certain information to buy-side analysts but not to sell-side analysts, or vice versa. Furthermore, a company should not discriminate among analysts in the provision of information or blackball particular analysts who have given negative reports on the company in the past.

Companies should consider issuing press releases prior to analyst meetings and conference calls and scripting those meetings and calls to decrease the chance that further information will be disclosed. If material nonpublic information is disclosed for the first time in an analyst meeting or call, the company should promptly issue a press release or otherwise make the information publicly available.

An information barrier commonly referred to as a "fire wall" is the most widely used approach to preventing the communication of material nonpublic information within firms. It restricts the flow of confidential information to those who need to know the information to perform their jobs effectively. The minimum elements of such a system include, but are not limited to, the following:

- substantial control of relevant interdepartmental communications, preferably through a clearance area within the firm in either the compliance or legal department;
- review of employee trading through the maintenance of "watch," "restricted," and "rumor" lists;
- documentation of the procedures designed to limit the flow of information between departments and of the enforcement actions taken pursuant to those procedures;
- heightened review or restriction of proprietary trading while a firm is in possession of material nonpublic information.

Although documentation requirements must, for practical reasons, take into account the differences between the activities of small firms and those of large, multi-service firms, firms of all sizes and types benefit by improving the documentation of their internal enforcement of fire wall procedures. Therefore, even at small firms, procedures concerning interdepartmental communication, the review of trading activity, and the investigation of possible violations should be compiled and formalized.

As a practical matter, to the extent possible, firms should consider the physical separation of departments and files to prevent the communication of sensitive information. For example, the investment-banking and corporate finance areas of a brokerage firm should be separated from the sales and research departments, and a bank's commercial lending department should be segregated from its trust and research departments.

There should be no overlap of personnel between such departments. A single supervisor or compliance officer should have the specific authority and responsibility to decide whether or not information is material and whether it is sufficiently public to be used as the basis for investment decisions. Ideally, the supervisor or compliance officer responsible for communicating information to a firm's research or brokerage area would not be a member of that area.

For a fire wall to be effective in a multi-service firm, an employee can be allowed to be on only one side of the wall at any given time. Inside knowledge may not be limited to information about a specific offering or a current financial condition of the company. Analysts may be exposed to a host of information about the company, including new product developments or future budget projections that clearly constitute inside knowledge and thus preclude the analyst from returning to his or her research function. For example, an analyst who follows a particular company may provide limited assistance to the investment bankers under carefully controlled circumstances when the firm's investment-banking department is involved in a deal with the company. That analyst must then be treated as though he or she were an investment banker; the analyst must remain on the investment-banking side of the wall until any information he or she learns is publicly disclosed. In short, the analyst cannot use any information learned in the course of the project for research purposes and cannot share that information with colleagues in the research department.

A primary objective of an effective fire wall procedure is to establish a reporting system in which authorized people review and approve communications between departments. If an employee behind a fire wall believes that he or she needs to share confidential information with someone on the other side of the wall, the employee should consult a designated compliance officer to determine whether sharing the information is necessary and how much information should be shared. If the sharing is necessary, the compliance officer should coordinate the process of "looking over the wall" so that the necessary information will be shared and the integrity of the procedure will be maintained.

An information barrier is the minimum procedure a firm should have in place to protect itself from liability. Firms should also consider restrictions or prohibitions on personal trading by employees and should carefully monitor both proprietary trading and personal trading by employees. Firms should require employees to make periodic reports (to the extent that such reporting is not already required by securities laws) of their own transactions and transactions made for the benefit of family members. Securities should be placed on a restricted list when a firm has or may have material nonpublic information. The broad distribution of a restricted list often triggers the sort of trading the list was developed to avoid. Therefore, a watch list shown to only the few people responsible for compliance should be used to monitor transactions in specified securities. The use of a watch list in combination with a restricted list is an increasingly common means of ensuring an effective procedure.

Multi-service firms should maintain written records of the communications between various departments. Firms should place a high priority on training and should consider instituting comprehensive training programs, particularly for employees in sensitive areas.

Procedures concerning the restriction or review of a firm's proprietary trading while it is in the possession of material nonpublic information will necessarily vary depending on the types of proprietary trading in which a firm may engage. A prohibition on all types of proprietary activity when a firm comes into possession of material nonpublic information is *not* appropriate. For example, when a firm acts as a market maker, a proprietary trading prohibition may be counterproductive to the goals of maintaining the confidentiality of information and market liquidity. This concern is particularly keen in the relationships between small, regional broker/dealers and small issuers. In many situations, a firm will take a small issuer public with the understanding that the firm will continue to be a market maker in the stock. In such instances, a withdrawal by the firm from market-making acts would be a clear tip to outsiders. However, firms that continue market-making activity while in the possession of material nonpublic information should instruct their market makers to remain passive to the market—that is, take only the contra side of unsolicited customer trades.

In risk-arbitrage trading, the case for a trading prohibition is more compelling. In contrast to market making, the impetus for arbitrage trading is neither passive nor reactive and the potential for illegal profits is greater. The most prudent course for firms is to suspend arbitrage activity when a security is placed on the watch list. Those firms that do continue arbitrage activity face a high hurdle in proving the adequacy of their internal procedures and must demonstrate stringent review and documentation of firm trades.

Written compliance policies and guidelines should be circulated to all employees of a firm. Policies and guidelines should be used in conjunction with training programs aimed at enabling employees to recognize material nonpublic information. As noted, material nonpublic information is not always clearly identifiable as such. Employees must be given sufficient training to either make an informed decision or consult a supervisor or compliance officer before engaging in questionable transactions.

APPLICATION OF THE STANDARD

Example 1. Frank Barnes, the president and controlling shareholder of the SmartTown clothing chain, decides to accept a proposed tender offer and sell the family business at a price almost double the market price of its shares. He describes this decision to his sister (SmartTown's treasurer), who conveys it to her daughter (who owns no stock in the family company at present), who tells her husband, Staple. Staple, however, tells his stockbroker, Alex Halsey, who immediately buys SmartTown stock for himself.

> *Comment:* The information regarding the pending sale is both material and nonpublic. Staple has violated Standard II(A) by communicating the inside information to his broker. Also, Halsey has violated the standard by initiating the transaction to buy the shares based on material nonpublic information.

Example 2. Josephine Walsh is riding an elevator up to her office when she overhears the chief financial officer (CFO) for the Swan Furniture Company tell the president of Swan that he has just calculated the company's earnings for the past quarter and they have unexpectedly and significantly dropped. The CFO adds that this drop will not be released to the public until next week. Walsh immediately calls her broker and tells him to sell her Swan stock.

> *Comment*: Walsh has sufficient information to determine that the information is both material and nonpublic. By trading on the inside information, she has violated Standard II(A).

Example 3. Samuel Peter, an analyst with Scotland and Pierce Incorporated, is assisting his firm with a secondary offering for Bright Ideas Lamp Company. Peter participates, via telephone conference call, in a meeting with Scotland and Pierce investment-banking employees and Bright Ideas' CEO. Peter is advised that the company's earnings projections for the next year have significantly dropped. Throughout the telephone conference call, several Scotland and Pierce salespeople and portfolio managers walk in and out of Peter's office, where the telephone call is taking place. As a result, they are aware of the drop in projected earnings for Bright Ideas. Before the conference call is concluded, the salespeople trade the stock of the company on behalf of the firm's clients and other firm personnel trade the stock in a firm proprietary account and in employee personal accounts.

> *Comment*: Peter violated Standard II(A) because he failed to prevent the transfer and misuse of material nonpublic information to others in his firm. Peter's firm should have adopted information barriers to prevent the communication of nonpublic information between departments of the firm. The salespeople and portfolio managers who traded on the information have also violated Standard II(A) by trading on inside information.

Example 4. Madison & Lambeau, a well-respected broker/dealer, submits a weekly column to Securities Weekly magazine. Once published, the column usually affects the value of the stocks discussed. Ron George, an employee of Madison & Lambeau, knows that Securities Weekly is published by Ziegler Publishing, for which his nephew is the night foreman. George's nephew faxes him an advance copy of the weekly column before it is printed. George regularly trades in the securities mentioned in the Madison & Lambeau column prior to its distribution, and to date, he has realized a personal profit of $42,000 as well as significant profits for his clients.

> *Comment*: George has violated Standard II(A) by trading on material non-public information. George's nephew has also violated the standard by communicating the information that causes George to trade.

Example 5. Greg Newman and his wife volunteer at a local charitable organization that delivers meals to the elderly. One morning, Newman's wife receives a telephone call from Betsy Sterling, another volunteer, who asks if Newman and his wife can fill in for her and her husband that afternoon. Mrs. Sterling indicates that her husband is busy at work because his company has just fired its chief financial officer for misappropriation of funds. Mrs. Newman agrees to perform the volunteer work for the Sterlings and advises her husband of the situation. Newman knows that Mr. Sterling is the CEO at O'Hara Brothers Incorporated. Newman determines that this information is not public and then sells his entire holding of 3,000 shares of O'Hara Brothers. Three days later, the firing is announced and O'Hara Brothers stock drops in value.

> *Comment:* Because the information is material and nonpublic, Newman has violated Standard II(A) by trading on this information.

Example 6. Elizabeth Levenson is based in Taipei and covers the Taiwanese market for her firm, which is based in Singapore. She is invited to meet the finance director of a manufacturing company along with the other 10 largest shareholders of the company. During the meeting, the finance director states that the company expects its workforce to strike next Friday, which will cripple productivity and distribution. Can Levenson use this information as a basis to change her rating on the company from "buy" to "sell"?

> *Comment:* Levenson must first determine whether the material information is public. If the company has not made this information public (a small-group forum does not qualify as a method of public dissemination), she cannot use the information according to Standard II(A).

Example 7. Leah Fechtman is trying to decide whether to hold or sell shares of an oil and gas exploration company that she owns in several of the funds she manages. Although the company has underperformed the index for some time already, the trends in the industry sector signal that companies of this type might become takeover targets. In the midst of the decision, her doctor, who casually follows the markets, mentions that she thinks that the company in question will soon be bought out by a large multinational conglomerate and that it would be a good idea to buy the stock right now. After talking to various investment professionals and checking their opinions on the company as well as industry trends, Fechtman decides the next day to accumulate more company stock.

> *Comment:* Although information on an expected takeover bid may be of the type that is generally material and nonpublic, in this case, the source of information is unreliable and could not be considered material. Therefore, Fechtman is not prohibited from trading the stock based on this information.

Example 8. Jagdish Teja is a buy-side analyst covering the furniture industry. Looking for an attractive company to recommend as a buy, he analyzed several furniture makers by studying their financial reports and visiting their operations. He also talked to some designers and retailers to find out which furniture styles are trendy and popular. Although none of the companies that he analyzed turned out to be a clear buy, he discovered that one of them, Swan Furniture Company (SFC), might be in trouble. Swan's extravagant new designs were introduced at substantial costs. Even though these designs initially attracted attention, in the long run, the public is buying more conservative furniture from other makers. Based on that and on P&L analysis, Teja believes that Swan's next-quarter earnings will drop substantially. He then issues a sell recommendation for SFC. Immediately after receiving that recommendation, investment managers start reducing the stock in their portfolios.

> *Comment*: Information on quarterly earnings figures is material and nonpublic. However, Teja arrived at his conclusion about the earnings drop based on public information and on pieces of nonmaterial nonpublic information (such as opinions of designers and retailers). Therefore, trading based on Teja's correct conclusion is not prohibited by Standard II(A).

Example 9. Roger Clement is a senior financial analyst who specializes in the European automobile sector at Rivoli Capital. Because he has been repeatedly nominated by many leading industry magazines and newsletters as "best analyst" for the automobile industry, he is widely regarded as an authority on the sector. After speaking with representatives of Turgot Chariots, a European auto manufacturer with sales primarily in Korea, as well as salespeople, labor leaders, his firm's Korean currency analysts, and banking officials, Clement reviewed his analysis of Turgot Chariots and concluded that (1) its newly introduced model will probably not meet sales anticipation, (2) its corporate restructuring strategy might well face serious opposition from the unions, (3) the depreciation of the Korean won should lead to pressure on margins for the industry in general and Turgot's market segment in particular, and (4) banks could take a tougher-than-expected stance in the soon-to-come round of credit renegotiations. For these reasons, he changed his recommendation from market overperform to underperform.

> *Comment*: To reach a conclusion about the value of the company, Clement has pieced together a number of nonmaterial or public bits of information that affect Turgot Chariots. Therefore, under the "mosaic theory," Clement has not violated Standard II(A) in drafting the report.

Example 10. The next day, Clement is preparing to be interviewed on a global financial news television program where he will discuss his changed recommendation on Turgot Chariots for the first time in public. While preparing for the program, he mentions to the show's producers and Mary Zito, the journalist who will be interviewing him, the information he will be discussing. Just prior to going on the air, Zito sells her holdings in Turgot Chariots.

> *Comment*: Zito knows that Clement's opinions will have a strong influence on the stock's behavior, so when she receives advanced notice of Clement's change of opinion, she knows it will have a material impact on the stock price, even if she is not totally aware of Clement's underlying reasoning. She is not a client of Clement but obtains early access to the material nonpublic information prior to publication. Her actions are thus trades based on material nonpublic information and violate Standard II(A).

Example 11. Timothy Holt is a portfolio manager for the Toro Aggressive Growth Fund, a large mutual fund with an aggressive growth mandate. As a result, the fund is heavily invested in small-cap companies with strong growth potential. Based on an unfavorable analysis of McCardell Industries by his research department, Holt decides to liquidate the fund's holdings in the company. Holt knows that this action will be widely viewed as negative by the market and that the company's stock is likely to plunge. He contacts several family members to tell them to liquidate any of their holdings before Toro's holdings are sold.

> *Comment:* Holt knows that Toro's trades have a strong influence on the market. Therefore, when he tells his family to sell stock in advance of Toro's trade, he has violated Standard II(A) by causing others to trade on material nonpublic information.

Example 12. Holt executes his sell order of McCardell Industries with Toro's broker, Karim Ahmed. Ahmed immediately recognizes the likely effect this order will have on the stock price of McCardell and sells his own holdings in the company prior to placing the order.

> *Comment:* Ahmed has violated Standard II(A) by trading on material non-public information.

Standard II: Integrity of Capital Markets

> ## (B) Market Manipulation
>
> Members and Candidates must not engage in practices that distort prices or artificially inflate trading volume with the intent to mislead market participants.

Guidance

Standard II(B) requires that members and candidates uphold market integrity by prohibiting market manipulation. Market manipulation includes practices that distort security prices or trading volume with the intent to deceive people or entities that rely on information in the market. Market manipulation damages the interests of all investors by disrupting the smooth functioning of financial markets and damaging investor confidence. Although it may be less likely to occur in more mature financial markets, cross-border investing increasingly exposes all global investors to the potential for such practices.

Market manipulation can be related to (1) transactions that deceive market participants by distorting the price-setting mechanism of financial instruments or (2) the dissemination of false or misleading information. The development of new products and technologies enhances the incentives, means, and opportunities for market manipulation.

Transaction-based manipulation includes but is not limited to:

- transactions that artificially distort prices or volume to give the impression of activity or price movement in a financial instrument and
- securing a controlling, dominant position in a financial instrument to exploit and manipulate the price of a related derivative and/or the underlying asset.

By requiring that violations include the intent to mislead by creating artificial price or volume levels, this standard is not meant to prohibit legitimate trading strategies that exploit a difference in market power, information, or other market inefficiencies. Legitimate orders in a thinly traded security could overwhelm the liquidity for that security, which would be different from efforts to artificially affect the price of the security at the close of trading. In addition, this standard is not meant to prohibit transactions done for tax purposes, such as selling and immediately buying back a particular stock. The intent of the action is critical to determining whether it is a violation of this standard.

Information-based manipulation includes, but is not limited to, spreading false rumors to induce trading by others. For example, members and candidates must refrain from "pumping up" the price of an investment by issuing misleading positive information or overly optimistic projections of a security's worth only to later "dump" ownership in the investment once the price of the stock, fueled by the misleading information's effect on other market participants, reaches an artificially high level.

Application of the Standard

Example 1. The principal owner of Financial Information Services (FIS) entered into an agreement with two microcap companies to promote the companies' stock in exchange for stock and cash compensation. The principal owner caused FIS to disseminate e-mails, design and maintain several Internet websites, and distribute an online investment newsletter–all of which recommended investment in the two companies. The systematic publication of purportedly independent analysis and recommendations containing inaccurate and highly promotional and speculative statements increased public investment in the companies and led to dramatically higher stock prices.

> *Comment*: The principal owner of FIS violated Standard II(B) by using inaccurate reporting and misleading information under the guise of independent analysis to artificially increase the stock price of the companies. Furthermore, the principal owner violated Standard V(A) by not having a reasonable and adequate basis for recommending the two companies and violated Standard IV(B) by not disclosing to investors the compensation agreements (which constituted a conflict of interest).

Example 2. An employee of a broker/dealer acquired a significant ownership interest in several publicly traded microcap stocks and held that stock in various brokerage accounts in which the broker/dealer had a controlling interest. The employee orchestrated the manipulation of the stock price by artificially increasing the bid price for the stock through transactions among the various accounts.

> *Comment*: The employee of the broker/dealer violated Standard II(B) by distorting the price of the stock through false trading and manipulative sales practices.

Example 3. Matthew Murphy is an analyst at Divisadero Securities & Co., which has a significant number of hedge funds among its most important brokerage clients. Two trading days before the publication of the quarter-end report, Murphy alerts his sales force that he is about to issue a research report on Wirewolf Semiconductor, which will include his opinion that

- quarterly revenues are likely to fall short of management's guidance,
- earnings will be as much as 5 cents per share (or more than 10 percent) below consensus, and
- Wirewolf's highly respected chief financial officer may be about to join another company.

Knowing that Wirewolf had already entered its declared quarter-end "quiet period" before reporting earnings (and thus would be reluctant to respond to rumors, etc.), Murphy times the release of his research report specifically to sensationalize the negative aspects of the message to create significant downward pressure on Wirewolf's stock to the distinct advantage of Divisadero's hedge fund clients. The report's conclusions are based on speculation, not on fact. The next day, the research report is broadcast to all of Divisadero's clients and to the usual newswire services.

Before Wirewolf's investor relations department can assess its damage on the final trading day of the quarter and refute Murphy's report, its stock opens trading sharply lower, allowing Divisadero's clients to cover their short positions at substantial gains.

> *Comment:* Murphy violated Standard II(B) by trying to create artificial price volatility designed to have material impact on the price of an issuer's stock. Moreover, by lacking an adequate basis for the recommendation, Murphy also violated Standard V(A).

Example 4. Rajesh Sekar manages two funds–an equity fund and a balanced fund–whose equity components are supposed to be managed following the same model. According to that model, the funds' holdings in stock CD are excessive. Reduction of CD holdings would not be easy because the stock has low liquidity in the stock market. Sekar decides to start trading larger portions of CD stock back and forth between his two funds to slowly increase the price, believing that market participants would see growing volume and increasing price and become interested in the stock. If other investors are willing to buy the CD stock because of such interest, then Sekar would be able to get rid of at least some part of his overweight position without inducing price decreases, so the whole transaction would be for the benefit of fund participants, even if additional brokers' commissions are accounted for.

> *Comment:* Sekar's plan would be beneficial for his funds' participants but is based on artificial distortion of both trading volume and price of CD stock and therefore constitutes a violation of Standard II(B).

Example 5. Sergei Gonchar is the chairman of the ACME Futures Exchange, which seeks to launch a new bond futures contract. In order to convince investors, traders, arbitragers, hedgers, and so on, to use its contract, the exchange attempts to demonstrate that it has the best liquidity. To do so, it enters into agreements with members so that they commit to a substantial minimum trading volume on the new contract over a specific period in exchange for substantial reductions on their regular commissions.

> *Comment:* Formal liquidity on a market is determined by the obligations set on market makers, but the actual liquidity of a market is better estimated by the actual trading volume and bid–ask spreads. Attempts to mislead participants on the actual liquidity of the market constitute a violation of Standard II(B). In this example, investors have been intentionally misled to believe they chose the most liquid instrument for some specific purpose and could eventually see the actual liquidity of the contract dry up suddenly after the term of the agreement if the "pump-priming" strategy fails. If ACME fully discloses its agreement with members to boost transactions over some initial launch

period, it does not violate Standard II(B). ACME's intent is not to harm investors but on the contrary to give them a better service. For that purpose, it may engage in a liquidity-pumping strategy, but it must be disclosed.

Example 6. Emily Gordon is a household products analyst employed by a research boutique, Picador & Co. Based on information that she has picked up during a trip through Latin America, she believes that Hygene, Inc., a major marketer of personal care products, has generated better-than-expected sales from its new product initiatives in South America. After modestly boosting her revenue and gross profit margin projections in her worksheet models for Hygene, Gordon estimates that her earnings projection of $2.00 per diluted share for the current year may be as much as 5 percent too low. She contacts the CFO of Hygene to try to gain confirmation of her findings from her trip and to get some feedback regarding her revised models. The CFO declines to comment and reiterates management's most recent guidance of $1.95 to $2.05 for the year.

Gordon decides to try to force a comment from the company by telling Picador & Co. clients who follow a momentum investment style that consensus earnings projections for Hygene are much too low, and that she's considering raising her published estimate by an ambitious $0.15 to $2.15 per share. She believes that, when word of an unrealistically high earnings projection filters back to Hygene's investor relations department, the company will feel compelled to update its earnings guidance. Meanwhile, Gordon hopes that she is at least correct with respect to the earnings direction and that she will help clients that act on her insights to profit from a quick gain trading on her advice.

> *Comment*: By exaggerating her earnings projections in order to try to fuel a quick gain in Hygene's stock price, Gordon is in violation of Standard II(B). Furthermore, by virtue of previewing to only a select group of clients her intentions of revising upward her earnings projections, she is in violation of Standard III(B). It would have been acceptable for Gordon to have instead written a report that
> - framed her earnings projection in a range of possible outcomes,
> - outlined clearly her assumptions used in her Hygene models that took into consideration the findings from her trip through Latin America, and
> - distributed the report to all Picador & Co. clients in an equitable manor.

Example 8. In an effort to pump up the price of his holdings in Moosehead & Belfast Railroad Company, Steve Weinberg logs on to several investor chat rooms on the Internet to start rumors that the company is about to expand its rail network in anticipation of receiving a large contract for shipping lumber.

> *Comment*: Weinberg has violated Standard II(B) by disseminating false information about Moosehead & Belfast with the intent to mislead market participants.

Standard III: Duties to Clients

(A) Loyalty, Prudence, and Care

Members and Candidates have a duty of loyalty to their clients and must act with reasonable care and exercise prudent judgment. Members and Candidates must act for the benefit of their clients and place their clients' interests before their employer's or their own interests. In relationships with clients, Members and Candidates must determine applicable fiduciary duty and must comply with such duty to persons and interests to whom it is owed.

Guidance

Standard III(A) clarifies that client interests are paramount. A member or candidate's responsibility to a client includes a duty of loyalty and a duty to exercise reasonable care. Investment actions must be carried out for the sole benefit of the client and in a manner the manager believes to be in the best interest of the client, given the known facts and circumstances. Members and candidates must exercise the same level of prudence, judgment, and care that they would apply in the management and disposition of their own interests under similar circumstances.

Prudence requires caution and discretion. The exercise of prudence by an investment professional requires that they must act with the care, skill, and diligence under the circumstances that a reasonable person acting in a like capacity and familiar with such matters would use. In the context of managing a client's portfolio, prudence requires following the investment parameters set forth by the client and balancing risk and return. Acting with care requires members and candidates to act in a prudent and judicious manner in avoiding harm to clients.

Standard III(A) also requires members and candidates to understand and adhere to any legally imposed fiduciary responsibility they assume with each client. Fiduciary duties are often imposed by law or regulation when an individual or institution is charged with the duty of acting for the benefit of another party, such as managing of investment assets. The duty required in fiduciary relationships exceeds what is acceptable in many other business relationships because the fiduciary is in an enhanced position of trust. Members and candidates must abide by any fiduciary duty legally imposed on them.

The first step for members and candidates in fulfilling their duty of loyalty to clients is to determine the identity of the "client" to whom the duty of loyalty is owed. In the context of an investment manager managing the personal assets of an individual, the client is easily identified. When the manager is responsible for the portfolios of pension plans or trusts, however, the client is not the person or entity who hires the manager but, rather, the beneficiaries of the plan or trust. The duty of loyalty is owed to the ultimate beneficiaries and not just the client.

Members and candidates must also be aware of whether they have "custody" or effective control of client assets. If so, a heightened level of responsibility arises. Members and candidates are considered to have custody if they have any direct or indirect access to client funds. Members and candidates must manage any pool of assets in their control in accordance with the terms of the governing documents (such as trust documents and investment management agreements), which are the primary determinant of the manager's powers and duties. Whenever their actions are contrary to provisions of those instruments or applicable law, members and candidates are exposed to potential violations of the standard.

Situations involving potential conflicts of interest with respect to responsibilities to clients can be extremely complex because they can involve a number of competing interests. The duty of loyalty, prudence, and care applies to a large number of persons in varying capacities, but the exact duties may differ in many respects, depending on the nature of the relationship with the client or the type of account under which the assets are managed. Members and candidates must put their obligation to clients first in all dealings. In addition, members and candidates should endeavor to avoid all real or potential conflicts of interest and forgo using opportunities for their own benefit at the expense of those to whom their duty of loyalty is owed.

The duty of loyalty, prudence, and care owed to the individual client is especially important because the professional investment manager typically possess greater knowledge than the client. This disparity places the individual client in a vulnerable position of trust. The manager in these situations should ensure that the client's objectives and expectations for the performance of the account are realistic and suitable to the client's circumstances and that the risks involved are appropriate. In most circumstances, recommended investment strategies should relate to the long-term objectives and circumstances of the client. Particular care must be taken to ensure that the goals of the investment manager or the firm in placing business, selling products, or executing security transactions do not conflict with the best interests and objectives of the client.

Members and candidates must follow any guidelines set out by their clients for the management of their assets. Some clients, such as charitable organizations and pension plans, have strict investment policies that limit investment options to certain types or classes of investments or prohibit investments in certain securities. Other organizations have aggressive policies that do not prohibit investments by type but instead set criteria on the basis of the portfolio's total risk and return.

Investment decisions may be judged in the context of the total portfolio rather than by individual investments within the portfolio. The member or candidate's duty is satisfied with respect to a particular investment if they have thoroughly considered the investment's place in the overall portfolio, the risk of loss and opportunity for gains, tax implications, and the diversification, liquidity, cash flow, and overall return requirements of the assets or the portion of the assets for which the manager is responsible.

The duty of loyalty, prudence and care can apply in a number of other situations faced by the investment professional other than with issues related directly to investing assets.

Part of a member or candidate's duty of loyalty includes voting proxies in an informed and responsible manner. Proxies have economic value to a client, and members and candidates must ensure that they properly safeguard and maximize this value. A fiduciary who fails to vote, casts a vote without considering the impact of the question, or votes blindly with management on nonroutine governance issues (e.g., a change in firm capitalization) may violate this standard. Voting of proxies is an integral part of the management of investments. A cost-benefit analysis may show that voting all proxies may not benefit the client, so voting proxies may not be necessary in all instances. Members and candidates should disclose to clients their proxy-voting policies.

An investment manager often has discretion over the selection of brokers executing transactions. Conflicts arise when an investment manager uses client brokerage to purchase research services that benefit the investment manager, a practice commonly called "soft dollars" or "soft commissions." Whenever a manager uses client brokerage to purchase goods or services that do not benefit the client, the manager should disclose to clients the method or policies followed by the manager in addressing the potential conflict. A manager who pays a higher commission than he or she would normally pay to purchase goods or services, without corresponding benefit to the client, violates the duty of loyalty to the client.

From time to time, a manager's client will direct the manager to use the client's brokerage to purchase goods or services for the client, a practice that is commonly called "directed brokerage." Because brokerage is an asset of the client and is used to benefit that client, not the manager, such practice does not violate any duty of loyalty. In such situations, the manager is obligated to seek best price and execution and be assured by the client that the goods or services purchased with brokerage will benefit the account beneficiaries and the manager should disclose to client that they may not be getting best execution.

Recommended Procedures for Compliance

Members and candidates with control of client assets should submit to each client, at least quarterly, an itemized statement showing the funds and securities in the custody or possession of the member or candidate, plus all debits, credits, and transactions that occurred during the period; disclose to the client where the assets are to be maintained, as well as where or when they are moved; and separate the client's assets from any other party's assets, including the member or candidate's own assets.

Members and candidates should review investments periodically to ensure compliance with the terms of the governing documents.

Members and candidates should establish policies and procedures with respect to proxy voting and the use of client brokerage, including soft dollars.

If a member or candidate is uncertain about the appropriate course of action with respect to a client, the member or candidate should ask what he or she would expect or demand if the member or candidate were the client. If in doubt, a member or candidate should disclose the questionable matter in writing and obtain client approval.

Members and candidates should address and encourage their firms to address the following topics when drafting their policies and procedures statements or manuals regarding responsibilities to clients:

- Follow all applicable rules and laws. Members and candidates must follow all legal requirements and applicable provisions of the CFA Institute Code of Ethics and Standards of Professional Conduct.

- Establish the investment objectives of the client. When taking investment actions, members and candidates must consider the appropriateness and suitability of the portfolio relative to (1) the client's needs and circumstances or (2) the investment's basic characteristics or (3) the basic characteristics of the total portfolio.

- Diversify. Members and candidates should diversify investments to reduce the risk of loss, unless diversification is not consistent with plan guidelines or is contrary to the account objectives.

- Deal fairly with all clients with respect to investment actions. Members and candidates must not favor some clients over others and should establish policies for allocating trades and disseminating investment recommendations.

- Disclose conflicts of interest. Members and candidates must disclose all actual and potential conflicts of interest so that clients can evaluate those conflicts.

- Disclose compensation arrangements. Members and candidates should make their clients aware of all forms of manager compensation.

- Vote proxies. Members and candidates should determine who is authorized to vote shares and vote proxies in the best interest of the clients and ultimate beneficiaries.

- Maintain confidentiality. Members and candidates must preserve the confidentiality of client information.

- Seek best execution. Members and candidates must seek best execution for their clients. Best execution refers to the trading process firms apply that seeks to maximize the value of a client's portfolio within the client's stated investment objectives and constraints.

- Place client interests first. Members and candidates must serve the best interest of the clients.

Applications

Example 1. First Country Bank serves as trustee for the Miller Company's pension plan. Miller is the target of a hostile takeover attempt by Newton, Inc. In attempting to ward off Newton, Miller's managers persuade Julian Wiley, an investment manager at First Country Bank, to purchase Miller common stock in the open market for the employee pension plan. Miller's officials indicate that such action would be favorably received and would probably result in other accounts being placed with the bank. Although Wiley believes the stock to be overvalued and would not ordinarily buy it, he purchases the stock to support Miller's managers, to maintain the company's good favor, and to realize additional new business. The heavy stock purchases cause Miller's market price to rise to such a level that Newton retracts its takeover bid.

> *Comment:* Standard III(A) requires that a member or candidate, in evaluating a takeover bid, act prudently and solely in the interests of plan participants and beneficiaries. To meet this requirement, a member or candidate must carefully evaluate the long-term prospects of the company against the short-term prospects presented by the takeover offer and by the ability to invest elsewhere. In this instance, Wiley, acting on behalf of his employer, the trustee, clearly violated Standard III(A) by using the profit-sharing plan to perpetuate existing management, perhaps to the detriment of plan participants and the company's shareholders, and to benefit himself. Wiley's responsibilities to the plan participants and beneficiaries should take precedence over any ties to corporate managers and self-interest. A duty exists to examine such a takeover offer on its own merits and to make an independent decision. The guiding principle is the appropriateness of the investment decision to the pension plan, not whether the decision benefits Wiley or the company that hired him.

Example 2. JNI, a successful investment counseling firm, serves as investment manager for the pension plans of several large, regionally based companies. Its trading activities generate a significant amount of commission-related business. JNI uses the brokerage and research services of many firms, but most of its trading activity is handled through a large brokerage company, Thompson, Inc., principally because of close personal relationships between the executives of the two firms. Thompson's commission structure is high in comparison with charges for similar brokerage services from other firms. JNI considers Thompson's research services and execution capabilities average. In exchange for JNI directing its brokerage to Thompson, Thompson absorbs a number of JNI overhead expenses, including those for rent.

Comment: JNI executives breached their fiduciary duty by using client brokerage for services that do not benefit JNI clients and by not obtaining best price and execution for their clients. Because JNI executives failed to uphold their duty of loyalty, they violated Standard III(A).

Example 3. Charlotte Everett, a struggling independent investment advisor, serves as investment manager for the pension plans of several companies. One of her brokers, Scott Company, is close to consummating management agreements with prospective new clients whereby Everett would manage the new client accounts and trade the accounts exclusively through Scott. One of Everett's existing clients, Crayton Corporation, has directed Everett to place securities transactions for Crayton's account exclusively through Scott. But to induce Scott to exert efforts to land more new accounts for her, Everett also directs transactions to Scott from other clients without their knowledge.

Comment: Everett has an obligation at all times to seek best price and execution on all trades. Everett may direct new client trades exclusively through Scott Company as long as Everett receives best price and execution on the trades or receives a written statement from new clients that she is not to seek best price and execution and that they are aware of the consequence for their accounts. Everett may trade other accounts through Scott as a reward for directing clients to Everett only if the accounts receive best price and execution and the practice is disclosed to the accounts. Because Everett did not disclose the directed trading, Everett has violated Standard III(A).

Example 4. Emilie Rome is a trust officer for Paget Trust Company. Rome's supervisor is responsible for reviewing Rome's trust account transactions and her monthly reports of personal stock transactions. Rome has been using Nathan Gray, a broker, almost exclusively for trust account brokerage transactions. Where Gray makes a market in stocks, he has been giving Rome a lower price for personal purchases and a higher price for sales than he gives to Rome's trust accounts and other investors.

Comment: Rome is violating her duty of loyalty to the bank's trust accounts by using Gray for brokerage transactions simply because Gray trades Rome's personal account on favorable terms.

Example 5. Lauren Parker, an analyst with Provo Advisors, covers South American equities for the firm. She likes to travel to the markets for which she is responsible and decides to go on a briefing trip to Chile, Argentina, and Brazil. The trip is sponsored by SouthAM, Inc., a research firm with a small broker/dealer affiliate that uses the clearing facilities of a larger New York brokerage house. SouthAM specializes in arranging South American trips for analysts during which they can meet with central bank officials, government ministers, local economists, and senior executives of corporations. SouthAM accepts commission dollars at a ratio of 2 to 1 against the hard-dollar cost of the research fee for the trip. Parker is not sure that SouthAM's execution is competitive but, without informing her supervisor, directs the trading desk at Provo to start giving commission business to SouthAM so she can take the trip. SouthAM has conveniently timed the briefing trip to coincide with the beginning of Carnival season, so Parker also decides to spend five days of vacation in Rio de Janeiro at the end of the trip. Parker used commission dollars to pay for the five days of hotel expenses.

> *Comment:* Parker violated Standard III(A) by not exercising her duty of loyalty her clients to determine whether the commissions charged by SouthAM were reasonable in relation to the benefit of the research provided by the trip and by not determining that best execution and prices can be received from SouthAM. In addition, the five extra days are not part of the research effort because they do not assist in the investment decision-making process and thus should not be paid for with client assets.

Example 6. Vida Knauss manages the portfolios of a number of high-net-worth individuals. A major part of her investment management fee is based on trading commissions. Knauss engages in extensive trading for each of her clients to ensure that she attains the minimum commission level set by her firm. While the securities purchased and sold for the clients are appropriate and fall within the acceptable asset classes for the clients, the amount of trading for each account exceeds what is necessary to accomplish the client's investment objectives.

> *Comment:* Knauss has violated Standard III(A) because she is using the assets of her clients to benefit her firm and herself.

Standard III: Duties to Clients

(B) Fair Dealing

Members and Candidates must deal fairly and objectively with all clients when providing investment analysis, making investment recommendations, taking investment action, or engaging in other professional activities.

Guidance

Standard III(B) requires members and candidates to treat all clients fairly when disseminating investment recommendations or material changes to prior investment advice or when taking investment action with regard to general purchases, new issues, or secondary offerings. Only through the fair treatment of all parties can the investment management profession maintain the confidence of the investing public.

When an investment advisor has multiple clients, the potential exists for the advisor to favor one client over another. This favoritism may take various forms, from the quality and timing of services provided to the allocation of investment opportunities. The term "fairly" implies that the member or candidate must take care not to discriminate against any clients when disseminating investment recommendations or taking investment action. Standard III(B) does not state "equally" because members and candidates could not possibly reach all clients at exactly the same time—whether by mail, telephone, computer, facsimile, or wire. Each client has unique needs, investment criteria, and investment objectives so that not all investment opportunities are suitable for all clients. In addition, members and candidates may provide more personal, specialized, or in-depth service to clients willing to pay for premium services through higher management fees or higher levels of brokerage. Members and candidates can differentiate their services to clients, but different levels of service must not disadvantage or negatively affect clients. In addition, the different service levels should be disclosed to clients and prospective clients and be available to everyone (i.e., different service levels should not be offered selectively).

Standard III(B) covers the conduct relating to two broadly defined categories of conduct—investment recommendations and investment action.

Investment recommendations. The first type of conduct involves members and candidates whose primary function is the preparation of investment recommendations to be disseminated either to the public or within a firm for the use of others in making investment decisions. This group includes members and candidates employed by investment counseling, advisory, or consulting firms as well as banks, brokerage firms, and insurance companies if the member or candidate's primary responsibility is the preparation of recommendations to be acted on by others, including those in the member or candidate's organization.

An investment recommendation is any opinion expressed by a member or candidate in regard to purchasing, selling, or holding a given security or other investment. This opinion can be disseminated to customers or clients through an initial detailed research report, through a brief update report, by addition to or deletion from a recommended list, or simply by oral communication. A recommendation that is distributed to anyone outside the organization is considered a communication for general distribution under Standard III(B).

Standard III(B) addresses the manner in which investment recommendations or changes in prior recommendations are disseminated to clients. Each member or candidate is obligated to ensure that information is disseminated in such a manner that all clients have a fair opportunity to act on every recommendation. Communicating with all clients on a uniform basis presents practical problems for members and candidates because of differences in timing and methods of communication with the various types of customers and clients. Members and candidates should encourage their firms to design an equitable system to prevent selective, discriminatory disclosure and should inform clients of what kind of communications they will receive.

The duty to clients imposed by Standard III(B) may be more critical when a member or candidate changes their recommendation than when they make an initial recommendation. Material changes in a member or candidate's prior investment advice arising from subsequent research should be communicated to all current clients, and particularly those clients who the member or candidate knows may have acted on or been affected by the earlier advice. Clients who don't know that the member or candidate has changed a recommendation and who therefore place orders contrary to a current recommendation should be advised of the changed recommendation before the order is accepted.

Investment actions. The second group includes those members and candidates whose primary function is taking investment action (portfolio management) based on research recommendations prepared internally or received from external sources. Investment action, like investment recommendations, can affect market value. Consequently, Standard III(B) requires that members or candidates treat all clients fairly in light of their investment objectives and circumstances. For example, when making investments in new offerings or in secondary financings, members and candidates should distribute the issues to all customers for whom the investments are appropriate in a manner consistent with the block-allocation policies of the firm. If the issue is oversubscribed, then the issue should be prorated to all subscribers. This action should be taken on a round-lot basis to avoid odd-lot distributions. In addition, if the issue is oversubscribed, members and candidates should forgo any sales to themselves or their immediate families to free up additional shares for clients.

Members and candidates must make every effort to treat all individual and institutional clients in a fair and impartial manner. A member or candidate may have multiple relationships with an institution; for example, a bank may hold many positions for a manager, such as corporate trustee, pension fund manager, manager of funds for individuals employed by the customer, loan originator, or creditor. A member or candidate must exercise care to treat clients fairly, including those with whom multiple relationships do not exist.

Members and candidates should disclose to clients and prospects the written allocation procedures they or their firms have in place and how the procedures would affect the client or prospect. The disclosure should be clear and complete so that the client can make an informed investment decision. Even when complete disclosure is made, however, members and candidates must put client interests ahead of their own. A member or candidate's duty of fairness and loyalty to clients can never be overridden by client consent to patently unfair allocation procedures.

Treating clients fairly also means that members and candidates should not take advantage of their position in the industry to the detriment of clients. For instance, in the context of IPOs, members and candidates must make bona fide public distributions of "hot issue" securities (defined as securities of a public offering that trade at a premium in the secondary market whenever such trading commences because of the great demand for the securities). Members and candidates are prohibited from withholding such securities for their own benefit and must not use such securities as a reward or incentive to gain benefit.

Recommended Procedures for Compliance

Although Standard III(B) refers to a member or candidate's responsibility to deal fairly and objectively with clients, members and candidates should also encourage their firms to establish compliance procedures requiring all employees who disseminate investment recommendations or take investment actions to treat customers and clients fairly. At the very least, a member or candidate should recommend appropriate procedures to management if none are in place and make management aware of possible violations of fair-dealing practices within the firm when they come to the attention of the member or candidate.

The extent of the formality and complexity of such compliance procedures depends on the nature and size of the organization and the type of securities involved. An investment advisor who is a sole proprietor and handles only discretionary accounts might not disseminate recommendations to the public, but that advisor should have formal written procedures to ensure that all clients receive fair investment action.

Good business practice dictates that initial recommendations be made available to all customers who indicate an interest. Although a member or candidate need not communicate a recommendation to all customers, the selection process by which customers receive information should be based on suitability and known interest, not on any preferred or favored status. A common practice to assure fair dealing is to communicate recommendations both within the firm and to customers—simultaneously.

Members and candidates should consider the following points when establishing fair-dealing compliance procedures:

Limit the number of people involved. Members and candidates should make reasonable efforts to limit the number of people who are privy to the fact that a recommendation is going to be disseminated.

Shorten the time frame between decision and dissemination. Members and candidates should make reasonable efforts to limit the amount of time that elapses between the decision to make an investment recommendation and the time the actual recommendation is disseminated. If a detailed institutional recommendation is in preparation that might take two or three weeks to publish, a short summary report including the conclusion might be published in advance. In an organization where both a research committee and investment policy committee must approve a recommendation, the meetings should be held on the same day if possible. The process of reviewing, printing, and mailing reports or faxing or distributing them by e-mail necessarily involves the passage of time, sometimes long periods of time. In large firms with extensive review processes, the time factor is usually not within the control of the analyst who prepares the report. Thus, many firms and their analysts communicate to customers and firm personnel the new or changed recommendations by an update or "flash" report. The communication technique might be fax, e-mail, wire, or short written report.

Publish personnel guidelines for pre-dissemination. Members and candidates should establish guidelines that prohibit personnel who have prior knowledge of an investment recommendation from discussing or taking any action on the pending recommendation.

Simultaneous dissemination. Members and candidates should establish procedures for dissemination of investment recommendations so that all clients are treated fairly—that is, with the goal of informing them at approximately the same time. For example, if a firm is going to announce a new recommendation, supervisory personnel should time the announcement to avoid placing any client or group of clients at unfair advantage relative to other clients. A communication to all branch offices should be sent at the time of the general announcement. When appropriate, the firm should accompany the announcement of a new recommendation with a statement that trading restrictions for the firm's employees are now in effect. The trading restrictions should stay in effect until the recommendation is widely distributed by communicating the information to all relevant clients. Once this has occurred, the member or candidate may follow up separately with individual clients, but members and candidates should not give favored clients advanced information when such pre-notification may disadvantage other clients.

Maintain a list of clients and their holdings. Members and candidates should maintain a list of all clients and the securities or other investments each client holds in order to facilitate notification of customers or clients of a change in an investment recommendation. If a particular security or other investment is to be sold, such a list could be used to ensure that all holders are treated fairly in the liquidation of that particular investment.

Develop written trade allocation procedures. When formulating procedures for allocating trades, members and candidates should develop a set of guiding principles that ensure

- fairness to advisory clients, both in priority of execution of orders and in the allocation of the price obtained in execution on block orders or trades;
- timeliness and efficiency in the execution of orders;
- accuracy of the member or candidate's records as to trade orders and client account positions.

With these principles in mind, members and candidates should develop or encourage their firm to develop written allocation procedures, with particular attention to procedures for block trades and new issues. Members and candidates should consider the following procedures:

- requiring orders and modifications or cancellations of orders to be in writing and time stamped;
- processing and executing orders on a first-in, first-out basis;
- developing a policy to address such issues as calculating execution prices and "partial fills" when trades are grouped, or blocked, for efficiency purposes;
- giving all client accounts participating in a block trade the same execution price and charging the same commission;
- when the full amount of the block order is not executed, allocating partially executed orders among the participating client accounts pro rata on the basis of order size;
- when allocating trades for new issues, obtaining advance indications of interest, allocating securities by client (rather than portfolio manager), and providing for a method for calculating allocations.

Disclose trade allocation procedures. Members and candidates should disclose to clients and prospective clients how they select accounts to participate in an order and how they determines the amount of securities each account will buy or sell. Trade allocation procedures must be fair and equitable, and disclosure of inequitable allocation methods does not relieve this obligation.

Establish systematic account review. Member and candidate supervisors should review each account on a regular basis to ensure that no client or customer is being given preferential treatment and that the investment actions taken for each account are suitable for the account's objectives. Because investments should be based on individual needs and circumstances, an investment manager may have good reasons for placing a given security or other investment in one account while selling it from another account. However, members and candidates should encourage firms to establish review procedures to detect whether trading in one account is being used to benefit a favored client.

Disclose levels of service. Members and candidates should disclose to all clients whether or not the organization offers different levels of service to clients for the same fee or different fees. Different levels of service should not be offered to clients selectively.

Applications

Example 1. Bradley Ames, a well-known and respected analyst, follows the computer industry. In the course of his research, he finds that a small, relatively unknown company whose shares are traded over the counter has just signed significant contracts with some of the companies he follows. After a considerable amount of investigation, Ames decides to write a research report on the company and recommend purchase. While the report is being reviewed by the company for factual accuracy, Ames schedules a luncheon with several of his best clients to discuss the company. At the luncheon, he mentions the purchase recommendation scheduled to be sent early the following week to all the firm's clients.

> *Comment:* Ames violated Standard III(B) by disseminating the purchase recommendation to the clients with whom he had lunch a week before the recommendation was sent to all clients.

Example 2. Spencer Rivers, president of XYZ Corporation, moves his company's growth-oriented pension fund to a particular bank primarily because of the excellent investment performance achieved by the bank's commingled fund for the prior five-year period. A few years later, Rivers compares the results of his pension fund with those of the bank's commingled fund. He is startled to learn that, even though the two accounts have the same investment objectives and similar portfolios, his company's pension fund has significantly underperformed the bank's commingled fund. Questioning this result at his next meeting with the pension fund's manager, Rivers is told that, as a matter of policy, when a new security is placed on the recommended list, Morgan Jackson, the pension fund manager, first purchases the security for the commingled account and then purchases it on a pro rata basis for all other pension fund accounts. Similarly, when a sale is recommended, the security is sold first from the commingled account and then sold on a pro rata basis from all other accounts. Rivers also learns that if the bank cannot get enough shares (especially the hot issues) to be meaningful to all the accounts, its policy is to place the new issues only in the commingled account.

Seeing that Rivers is neither satisfied nor pleased by the explanation, Jackson quickly adds that nondiscretionary pension accounts and personal trust accounts have a lower priority on purchase and sale recommendations than discretionary pension fund accounts. Furthermore, Jackson states, the company's pension fund had the opportunity to invest up to 5 percent in the commingled fund.

> *Comment:* The bank's policy did not treat all customers fairly, and Jackson violated her duty to her clients by giving priority to the growth-oriented commingled fund over all other funds and to discretionary accounts over nondiscretionary accounts. Jackson must execute orders on a systematic basis that is fair to all clients. In addition, trade allocation procedures should be disclosed to all clients from the beginning. Of course, in this case, disclosure of the bank's policy would not change the fact that the policy is unfair.

Example 3. Dominic Morris works for a small regional securities firm. His work consists of corporate finance activities and investing for institutional clients. Arena, Ltd., is planning to go public. The partners have secured rights to buy a arena football league franchise and are planning to use the funds from the issue to complete the purchase. Because arena football is the current rage, Morris believes he has a hot issue on his hands. He has quietly negotiated some options for himself for helping convince Arena to do the financing. When he seeks expressions of interest, the institutional buyers oversubscribe the issue. Morris, assuming that the institutions have the financial clout to drive the stock up, then fills all orders (including his own) and cuts back the institutional blocks.

> *Comment:* Morris has violated Standard III(B) by not treating all customers fairly. He should not have taken any shares himself and should have prorated the shares offered among all clients. In addition, he should have disclosed to his firm and to his clients that he had received options as part of the deal [see Standard VI(A)].

Example 4. Eleanor Preston, the chief investment officer of Porter Williams Investments (PWI), a medium-sized money management firm, has been trying to retain a difficult client, Colby Company. Management at the disgruntled client, which accounts for almost half of PWI's revenues, recently told Preston that if the performance of its account did not improve, it would find a new money manager. Shortly after this threat, Preston purchases mortgage-backed securities (MBS) for several accounts, including Colby's. Preston is busy with a number of transactions that day, so she fails to allocate the trades immediately or write up the trade tickets. A few days later, when Preston is allocating trades, she notes that some of the MBS have significantly increased in price and some have dropped. Preston decides to allocate the profitable trades to Colby and spread the losing trades among several other PWI accounts.

Comment: Preston violated Standard III(B) by failing to deal fairly with her clients in taking these investment actions. Preston should have allocated the trades prior to executing the orders, or she should have had a systematic approach to allocating the trades, such as pro rata, as soon after they were executed as practicable. Among other things, Preston must disclose to the client that the advisor may act as broker for, receive commissions from, and have a potential conflict of interest regarding both parties in agency cross-transactions. After the disclosure, she should obtain from the client consent authorizing such transactions in advance.

Example 5. Saunders Industrial Waste Management (SIWM) publicly indicates to analysts that it is comfortable with the somewhat disappointing earnings per share projection of $1.15 for the quarter. Bernard Roberts, an analyst at Coffey Investments, is confident that SIWM management has understated the forecasted earnings so that the real announcement would cause an "upside surprise" and boost the price of SIWM stock. The "whisper number" estimate based on extensive research and discussed among knowledgeable analysts is higher than $1.16. Saunders repeats the $1.16 figure in his research report to all Coffey clients but informally tells his larger clients that he expects the earnings per share to be higher, making SIWM a good buy.

Comment: By not sharing his opinion regarding the potential for a significant upside earnings surprise with all clients, Roberts is not treating all clients fairly and has violated Standard III(B).

Example 6. Jenpin Weng uses e-mail to issues a new recommendation to all his clients. He then calls his three biggest institutional clients to discuss the recommendation in detail.

Comment: Weng has not violated Standard III(B) because he widely disseminated the recommendation and provided the information to all his clients prior to discussing it with a select few. Weng's larger clients received additional personal service that they presumably pay for through bigger fees or because they have a large amount of assets under Weng's management. Weng would have violated Standard III(B) if he had discussed the report with a select group of clients prior to distributing it to all his clients.

Standard III: Duties to Clients

(C) Suitability

1. When Members and Candidates are in an advisory relationship with a client, they must:

   a. Make a reasonable inquiry into a client or prospective client's investment experience, risk and return objectives, and financial constraints prior to making any investment recommendation or taking investment action and must reassess and update this information regularly.

   b. Determine that an investment is suitable to the client's financial situation and consistent with the client's written objectives, mandates, and constraints before making an investment recommendation or taking investment action.

   c. Judge the suitability of investments in the context of the client's total portfolio.

2. When Members and Candidates are responsible for managing a portfolio to a specific mandate, strategy, or style, they must only make investment recommendations or take investment actions that are consistent with the stated objectives and constraints of the portfolio.

Guidance

Standard III(C) requires that members and candidates who are in an investment advisory relationship with clients consider carefully the needs, circumstances, and objectives of the clients when determining the appropriateness and suitability of a given investment or course of investment action.

The responsibilities conferred upon members and candidates to gather information and make a suitability analysis prior to making a recommendation or taking investment action falls on those members and candidates who provide investment advice in the course of an advisory relationship with a client. Other members and candidates often are simply executing specific instructions for retail clients when buying or selling securities, such as shares in mutual funds. These members and candidates and others, such as sell-side analysts, may not have the opportunity to judge the suitability of the particular investment for the person or entity. In cases of unsolicited trade requests that a member or candidate knows are unsuitable for the client, the member or candidate should refrain from making the trade or seek an affirmative statement from the client that suitability is not a consideration.

When an advisory relationship exists, members and candidates must gather client information at the inception of the relationship. Such information includes the client's financial circumstances, personal data (such as age and occupation) that are relevant to investment decisions, attitudes toward risk, and objectives in investing. This information should be incorporated into a written investment policy statement (IPS) that addresses the client's risk tolerance, return requirements, and all investment constraints (including time horizon, liquidity needs, tax concerns, legal and regulatory factors, and unique circumstances). Without identifying such client factors, members and candidates cannot judge whether a particular investment or strategy is suitable for a particular client. The IPS also should identify and describe the roles and responsibilities of the parties to the advisory relationship and investment process, as well as schedules for review and evaluation. After formulating long-term capital market expectations, members and clients can assist in developing an appropriate strategic asset allocation and investment program for the client, whether these are presented in separate documents or incorporated in the IPS or in appendices to the IPS.

Such an inquiry should be repeated at least annually and prior to material changes to any specific investment recommendations or decisions on behalf of the client. The effort to determine the needs and circumstances of each client is not a one-time occurrence. Investment recommendations or decisions are usually part of an ongoing process that takes into account the diversity and changing nature of portfolio and client characteristics. The passage of time is bound to produce changes that are important with respect to investment objectives.

For an individual client, such changes might include the number of dependents, personal tax status, health, liquidity needs, risk tolerance, the amount of wealth beyond that represented in the portfolio, and the extent to which compensation and other income provide for current income needs. With respect to an institutional client, such changes might relate to the magnitude of unfunded liabilities in a pension fund, the withdrawal privileges in an employee's savings plan, or the distribution requirements of a charitable foundation. Without efforts to update information concerning client factors, one or more factors could change without the investment manager's knowledge.

Suitability review can be done effectively only if the client fully discloses his or her complete financial portfolio, including those portions not managed by the member or candidate. If clients withhold information about their financial portfolio, the suitability analysis conducted by members and candidates can not be expected to be complete but must be done based on the information provided.

One of the most important factors to be considered in matching appropriateness and suitability of an investment with a client's needs and circumstances is measuring that client's tolerance for risk. The investment professional must consider the possibilities of rapidly changing investment environments and their likely impact on a client's holdings, both individual securities and the collective portfolio. The risk of many investment strategies can and should be analyzed and quantified in advance.

The use of synthetic investment vehicles and derivative investment products has introduced particular issues of risk. Members and candidates should pay careful attention to the leverage often inherent in such vehicles or products when considering them for use in a client's investment program. Such leverage and limited liquidity, depending on the degree to which they are hedged, bear directly on the issue of suitability for the client.

The investment profession has long recognized that the combination of several different investments is likely to provide a more acceptable level of risk exposure than having all assets in a single investment. The unique characteristics (or risks) of an individual investment may become partially or entirely neutralized when combined with other individual investments within a portfolio. Some reasonable amount of diversification is the norm for many portfolios, especially those managed by individuals or institutions that have some degree of fiduciary responsibility. An investment with high relative risk on its own may be a suitable investment in the context of the entire portfolio or when the client's stated objectives contemplate speculative or risky investments. It may be the case that the manager is responsible for only a portion of the client's total portfolio or that the client has not provided the full financial picture of the client to the manager. Members and candidates can be responsible only for assessing suitability of a investment given the information and criteria provided by the clients.

Some members and candidates do not manage money for individuals but are responsible for managing a fund to an index or an expected mandate. In those cases, the member or candidate's responsibility is to invest consistent with the stated mandate. For example, a member or candidate who serves as the fund manager for a large-cap income fund would not be following the fund mandate by investing heavily in small-cap or start-up companies whose stock is speculative in nature. Members and candidates who manage pooled assets to a specific mandate are not responsible for determining the suitability of the fund as an investment for investors who may be purchasing shares in the fund. The responsibility for determining the suitability of an investment for clients can only be conferred on members and candidates who have an advisory relationship with clients.

Recommended Procedures for Compliance

To fulfill the basic provisions of Standard III(C), a member or candidate should put the needs and circumstances of each client and the client's investment objectives into a written investment policy statement (IPS) for each client. In formulating an investment policy for the client, the member or candidate should take the following into consideration:

- Client identification–(1) type and nature of clients, (2) the existence of separate beneficiaries, and (3) approximate portion of total client assets;
- Investor objectives–(1) return objectives (income, growth in principal, maintenance of purchasing power) and (2) risk tolerance (suitability, stability of values).
- Investor constraints–(1) liquidity needs, (2) expected cash flows (patterns of additions and/or withdrawals), (3) investable funds (assets and liabilities or other commitments), (4) time horizon, (5) tax considerations, (6) regulatory and legal circumstances, (7) investor preferences, prohibitions, circumstances, and unique needs, and (8) proxy-voting responsibilities and guidance.
- Performance measurement benchmarks.

The investor's objectives and constraints should be maintained and reviewed periodically to reflect any changes in the client's circumstances. Members and candidates should regularly compare client constraints with capital market expectations to arrive at an appropriate asset allocation. Changes in either factor may result in a fundamental change in asset allocation. Annual review is reasonable unless business or other reasons, such as a major change in market conditions, dictate more frequent review. Members and candidates should document attempts at such a review if circumstances prevent it.

Applications

Example 1. Caleb Smith, an investment advisor, has two clients: Larry Robertson, 60 years old, and Gabriel Lanai, 40 years old. Both clients earn roughly the same salary, but Robertson has a much higher risk tolerance because he has a large asset base. Robertson is willing to invest part of his assets very aggressively; Lanai wants only to achieve a steady rate of return with low volatility to pay for his children's education. Smith recommends investing 20 percent of both portfolios in zero-yield small-cap high-technology issues.

> *Comment:* In Robertson's case, the investment may be appropriate given his financial circumstances and aggressive investment position but, this investment would not be suitable for Lanai. Smith would violate Standard III(C) by applying Robertson's investment strategy to Lanai because Lanai's financial circumstances and objectives are different.

Example 2. Jessica Walters, an investment advisor, suggests to Brian Crosby, a risk-averse client, that covered call options be used in his equity portfolio. The purpose would be to enhance Crosby's income and partially offset any untimely depreciation in value should the stock market or other circumstances affect his holdings unfavorably. Walters educates Crosby about all possible outcomes, including the risk of incurring an added tax liability if a stock rises in price and is called away and, conversely, the risk of his holdings losing protection on the downside if prices drop sharply.

> *Comment:* When determining suitability of an investment, the primary focus should be on the characteristics of the client's entire portfolio, not on an issue-by-issue analysis. The basic characteristics of the entire portfolio will largely determine whether the investment recommendations are taking client factors into account. Therefore, the most important aspects of a particular investment will be those that will affect the characteristics of the total portfolio. In this case, Walters properly considered the investment in the context of the entire portfolio and thoroughly explained the investment to the client.

Example 3. In a regular meeting with Seth Jones, the portfolio managers at Blue Chip Investment Advisors are careful to allow some time to review his current needs and circumstances. In doing so, they learn that some significant changes have recently taken place. A wealthy uncle left Jones an inheritance that increased his net worth fourfold, to $1,000,000.

> *Comment:* The inheritance significantly increased Jones's ability and possibly his willingness to assume risk and diminished the average yield required to meet his current income needs. Jones financial circumstances have definitely changed, so Blue Chip managers must update Jones' investment policy statement to understand how his investment objectives have changed. Accordingly, the Blue Chip portfolio managers should consider a somewhat higher equity ratio for his portfolio than was called for by the previous circumstances, and the managers' specific common stock recommendations might be heavily tilted toward low-yield, growth-oriented issues.

Example 4. Louis Perkowski manages a high-income mutual fund. He purchases zero-dividend stock in a financial services company because he believes the stock is undervalued and is in a potential growth industry, making it an attractive investment.

> *Comment:* A zero-dividend stock does not seem to fit the mandate of the fund that Perkowski is managing. Unless, Perkowski's investment fits within the mandate or is within the realm of investments allowable under the disclosures of the fund, Perkowski has violated Standard III(C).

Example 5. Max Gubler, CIO of a property/casualty insurance subsidiary of a large financial conglomerate, wants to better diversify the company's investment portfolio and increase its returns. The company's investment policy statement (IPS) provides for highly liquid investments, such as large caps, governments, and supra-nationals, as well as corporate bonds with a minimum credit rating of AA– and maturity of no more than five years. In a recent presentation, a venture capital group offered very attractive prospective returns on some of their private equity funds providing seed capital. An exit strategy is already contemplated but investors will first have to observe a minimum three-year lock-up period, with a subsequent laddered exit option for a maximum of one third of shares per year. Gubler does not want to miss this opportunity and after an extensive analysis and optimization of this asset class with the company's current portfolio, he invests 4 percent in this seed fund, leaving the portfolio's total equity exposure still well below its upper limit.

> *Comment:* Gubler violates standards III(A) and III(C). His new investment locks up part of the company's assets for at least three and for up to as many as five years and possibly beyond. Since the IPS requires investments in highly liquid investments and describes accepted asset classes, private equity investments with a lock-up period certainly do not qualify. Even without

such lock-up periods an asset class with only an occasional, and thus implicitly illiquid, market may not be suitable. Although an IPS typically describes objectives and constraints in great detail, the manager must make every effort to understand the client's business and circumstances. Doing so should also enable the manager to recognize, understand, and discuss with the client other factors that may be or may become material in the investment management process.

Standard III: Duties to Clients

(D) Performance Presentation

When communicating investment performance information, Members and Candidates must make reasonable efforts to make sure that it is fair, accurate, and complete.

Guidance

Standard III(D) requires members and candidates to provide credible performance information to clients and prospective clients and to avoid misstating performance or misleading clients and prospective clients about the investment performance of members or candidates or their firms. This standard encourages full disclosure of investment performance data to clients and prospective clients.

Standard III(D) covers any practice that would lead to misrepresentation of a member or candidate's performance record, whether the practice involves performance presentation or performance measurement. This standard prohibits misrepresentations of past performance or reasonably expected performance. A member or candidate must give a fair and complete presentation of performance information whenever communicating data with respect to the performance history of individual accounts, composites or groups of accounts, or composites of an analyst or firm's performance results. Further, members and candidates should not state or imply that clients will obtain or benefit from a rate of return that was generated in the past.

The requirements of this standard are not limited to members and candidates managing separate accounts. Anytime a member or candidate provides performance information for which the manager is claiming responsibility, such as for pooled funds, the history must be accurate. Research analysts promoting the success or accuracy of their recommendations must ensure that their claims are fair, accurate, and complete.

If the presentation is brief, the member or candidate must make available to clients and prospects, upon request, the detailed information supporting that communication.

Recommended Procedures for Compliance

For members and candidates seeking to show the performance history of the assets they manage, compliance with the Global Investment Performance Standards (GIPS) is the best method to meet their obligations under Standard III(D). Members and candidates should encourage their firms to adhere to the GIPS standards.

Members and candidates can also meet their obligations under Standard III(D) by
- considering the knowledge and sophistication of the audience to whom a performance presentation is addressed,

- presenting the performance of the weighted composite of similar portfolios rather than using a single representative account,
- including terminated accounts as part of performance history,
- including disclosures that would fully explain the performance results being reported (for example, stating, when appropriate, that results are simulated when model results are used, clearly indicating when the performance record is that of a prior entity, or disclosing whether the performance is gross of fees, net of fees, or after tax),
- maintaining the data and records used to calculate the performance being presented.

Applications

Example 1. Kyle Taylor of Taylor Trust Company, noting the performance of Taylor's common trust fund for the past two years, states in a brochure sent to his potential clients that "You can expect steady 25 percent annual compound growth of the value of your investments over the year." Taylor Trust's common trust fund did increase at the rate of 25 percent per annum for the past year which mirrored the increase of the entire market. The fund, however, never averaged that growth for more than one year, and the average rate of growth of all of its trust accounts for five years was 5 percent per annum.

> *Comment:* Taylor's brochure is in violation of Standard III(D). Taylor should have disclosed that the 25 percent growth occurred only in one year. Additionally, Taylor did not include client accounts other than those in the firm's common trust fund. A general claim of firm performance should take into account the performance of all categories of accounts. Finally, by stating that clients can expect a steady 25 percent annual compound growth rate, Taylor also violated Standard I(C), which prohibits statements of assurances or guarantees regarding an investment.

Example 2. Anna Judd, a senior partner of Alexander Capital Management, circulates a performance sheet listing performance figures for capital appreciation accounts for the years 1988 through 2004, and claiming compliance with the Global Investment Performance Standards (GIPS). Returns are not calculated in accordance with the Global Investment Performance Standards (GIPS) because the composites are not asset weighted, which is a violation of GIPS.

> *Comment:* Judd is in violation of Standard III(D). When claiming compliance with GIPS, firms must meet all the requirements and mandatory disclosures and any other additional requirements or disclosures necessary to that firm's specific situation. Judd's violation is not from any misuse of the data but from a false claim of GIPS compliance.

Example 3. Aaron McCoy is vice president and managing partner of the equity investment group of Mastermind Financial Advisors, a new business. Mastermind recruited McCoy because he had a proven six-year track record with G&P

Financial. In developing Mastermind's advertising and marketing campaign, McCoy prepared an advertisement that included the equity investment performance he achieved at G&P Financial. The advertisement for Mastermind did not identify the equity performance as being earned while at G&P. The advertisement was distributed to existing clients and prospective clients of Mastermind.

> *Comment*: McCoy violated Standard III(D) by distributing an advertisement that contained material misrepresentations regarding the historical performance of Mastermind. Standard III(D) requires that members and candidates make every reasonable effort to ensure that performance information is a fair, accurate, and complete representation of an individual or firm's performance. As a general matter, this standard does not prohibit showing past performance of funds managed at a prior firm as part of a performance track record so long as it is accompanied by appropriate disclosures detailing where the performance comes from and the person's specific role in achieving that performance. If McCoy chooses to use his past performance from G&P in Mastermind's advertising, he should make full disclosure as to the source of the historical performance.

Example 4. Jed Davis developed a mutual fund selection product based on historical information from the 1990–95 period. Davis tested his methodology by applying it retroactively to data from the 1996–2003 period, thus producing simulated performance results for those years. In January 2004, Davis's employer decided to offer the product and Davis began promoting it through trade journal advertisements and direct dissemination to clients. The advertisements included the performance results for the 1996–2003 period but did not indicate that the results were simulated.

> *Comment*: Davis violated Standard III(D) by failing to clearly identify simulated performance results. Standard III(D) prohibits members and candidates from making any statements that misrepresent the performance achieved by them or their firms and requires members and candidates to make every reasonable effort to ensure that performance information presented to clients is fair, accurate, and complete. Use of the simulated results should be accompanied by full disclosure as to the source of the performance data, including the fact that the results from 1995 through 2003 were the result of applying the model retroactively to that time period.

Example 5. In a presentation prepared for prospective clients, William Kilmer shows the rates of return realized over a five-year period by a "composite" of his firm's discretionary accounts with a balanced objective. This "composite," however, consisted of only a few of the accounts that met the balanced criteria set by the firm, excluded accounts under a certain asset level without disclosing the fact of their exclusion, and included nonbalanced accounts that would boost investment results. In addition, to achieve better results, Kilmer manipulated the narrow range of accounts included in the composite by changing the accounts that made up the composite over time.

Comment: Kilmer violated Standard III(D) by misrepresenting the facts in the promotional material sent to prospective clients, distorting his firm's performance record, and failing to include disclosure that would have clarified the presentation.

Standard III: Duties to Clients

(E) Preservation of Confidentiality

Members and Candidates must keep information about current, former, and pro-spective clients confidential unless:

1. The information concerns illegal activities on the part of the client;
2. Disclosure is required by law; or
3. The client or prospective client permits disclosure of the information.

Guidance

Standard III(E) requires that members and candidates to preserve the confidentiality of information communicated to them by their clients, prospective clients, and former clients. This standard is applicable when (1) the member or candidate receives information on the basis of his or her special ability to conduct a portion of the client's business or personal affairs and (2) the member or candidate receives information that arises from or is relevant to that portion of the client's business that is the subject of the special or confidential relationship. If disclosure of the information is required by law or the information concerns illegal activities by the client, however, the member or candidate may have an obligation to report the activities to the appropriate authorities.

As a general matter, members and candidates must comply with applicable law. If applicable law requires disclosure of client information in certain circumstances, members and candidates must comply with the law. Similarly, if applicable law requires members and candidates to maintain confidentiality, even if the information concerns illegal activities on the part of the client, members and candidates should not disclose such information. When in doubt, members and candidates should consult with their employer's compliance personnel or outside counsel before disclosing confidential information about clients.

This standard protects the confidentiality of client information even if the person or entity is no longer a client of the member or candidate. Therefore, members and candidates must continue to maintain the confidentiality of client records even after the client relationship has ended. However, if a client or former client expressly authorizes the member or candidate to disclose information, the member or candidate may follow the terms of the authorization and provide the information.

Professional Conduct Investigations by CFA Institute. The requirements of Standard III(E) are not intended to prevent members and candidates from cooperating with an investigation by CFA Institute's Professional Conduct Program (PCP). When permissible under applicable law, members and candidates shall consider the PCP an extension of themselves when requested to provide information about a client in support of a PCP investigation into their own conduct. Members and candidates are encouraged to cooperate with investigations into the conduct of others. Any information turned over to the PCP is kept in the strictest confidence. Members and candidates will not be considered in violation of this standard by forwarding confidential information to the PCP.

Recommended Procedures for Compliance

The simplest, most conservative, and most effective way to comply with Standard III(E) is to avoid disclosing any information received from a client except to authorized fellow employees who are also working for the client. In some instances, however, a member or candidate may want to disclose information received from clients that is outside the scope of the confidential relationship and does not involve illegal activities. Before making such a disclosure, a member or candidate should ask the following:

*   In what context was the information disclosed? If disclosed in a discussion of work being performed for the client, is the information relevant to the work?
*   Is the information background material that, if disclosed, will enable the member or candidate to improve service to the client?

Applications

Example 1. Sarah Connor, a financial analyst employed by Johnson Investment Counselors, Inc., provides investment advice to the trustees of City Medical Center. The trustees have given her a number of internal reports concerning City Medical's needs for physical plant renovation and expansion. They have asked Connor to recommend investments that would generate capital appreciation in endowment funds to meet projected capital expenditures. Connor is approached by a local businessman, Thomas Kasey, who is considering a substantial contribution either to City Medical Center or to another local hospital. Kasey wants to find out the building plans of both institutions before making a decision, but he does not want to speak to the trustees.

> *Comment*: The trustees gave Connor the internal reports so she could advise them on how to manage their endowment funds. Because the information in the reports is clearly both confidential and within the scope of the confidential relationship, Standard III(E) requires that Connor refuse to divulge information to Kasey.

Example 2. Lynn Moody is an investment officer at the Lester Trust Company. She has an advisory customer who has talked to her about giving approximately $50,000 to charity to reduce her income taxes. Moody is also treasurer of the Home for Indigent Widows (HIW), which is planning its annual giving campaign. HIW hopes to expand its list of prospects, particularly those capable of substantial gifts. Moody recommends that HIW's vice president for corporate gifts call on her customer and ask for a donation in the $50,000 range.

Comment: Even though the attempt to help the Home for Indigent Widows was well intended, Moody violated Standard III(E) by revealing confidential information about her client.

Example 3. Government officials approach Casey Samuel, the portfolio manager for Garcia Company's pension plan, to examine pension fund records. They tell her that Garcia's corporate tax returns are being audited and the pension fund reviewed. Two days earlier Samuel learned in a regular investment review meeting with Garcia officers that potentially excessive and improper charges are being made to the pension plan by Garcia. Samuel consults her employer's general counsel and is advised that Garcia has probably violated tax and fiduciary regulations and laws.

Comment: Samuel should inform her supervisor of these activities, and her employer should take steps, with Garcia, to remedy the violations. If that approach is not successful, Samuel and her employer should seek advice of legal counsel to determine the appropriate steps to be taken. Samuel may well have a duty to disclose the evidence she has of the continuing legal violations and to resign as asset manager for Garcia.

Example 4. David Bradford manages money for a family-owned real estate development corporation. He also manages the individual portfolios of several of the family members and officers of the corporation, including the chief financial officer (CFO). Based on the financial records from the corporation, as well as some questionable practices of the CFO that he has observed, Bradford believes that the CFO is embezzling money from the corporation and putting it into his personal investment account.

Comment: Bradford should check with his firm's compliance department as well as outside counsel to determine whether applicable securities regulations require reporting the CFO's financial records.

Standard IV: Duties to Employers

(A) Loyalty

In matters related to their employment, Members and Candidates must act for the benefit of their employer and not deprive their employer of the advantage of their skills and abilities, divulge confidential information, or otherwise cause harm to their employer.

Guidance

Standard IV(A) requires members and candidates to protect the interests of their firm by refraining from any conduct that would injure the firm, deprive it of profit, or deprive it of the advantage of the member or candidate's skills and ability. Members and candidates must always place the interests of clients above the interests of their employer. Otherwise, in matters related to their employment, members and candidates must not engage in conduct that harms the interests of the employer. Implicit in this standard is the obligation of members and candidates to comply with the policies and procedures established by their employers that govern the employer–employee relationship–to the extent that such policies and procedures do not conflict with applicable laws, rules, regulations, or the Code and Standards.

This standard is not meant to be a blanket requirement to place employer interests ahead of personal interests in all matters. This standard does not require members and candidates to subordinate important personal and family obligations to their work. Members and candidates should enter into a dialogue with their employer about balancing personal and employment obligations when personal matters may interfere with their work on a regular or significant basis.

In addition, the employer–employee relationship imposes duties and responsibilities on both parties. Employers must adhere to the duties and responsibilities that they owe to their employees if they expect to have contented and productive employees.

Independent Practice. Included in Standard IV(A) is the requirement that members and candidates abstain from independent competitive activity that could conflict with the interests of their employer. Although standard IV(A) does not preclude members or candidates from entering into an independent business while still employed, members and candidates who plan to engage in independent practice for compensation must provide notification to their employer describing the types of service the members or candidates will render to prospective independent clients, the expected duration of the services, and the compensation for the services. Members and candidates should not render services until receiving consent from their employer to all of the terms of the arrangement.

"Practice" means any service that the employer currently makes available for remuneration. "Undertaking independent practice" means engaging in competitive business, as opposed to making preparations to begin such practice.

Leaving an Employer. When investment professionals plan to leave their current employer, they must continue to act in the employer's best interest, and must not engage in any activities that would conflict with this duty until their resignation becomes effective. It is difficult to define specific guidelines for those members and candidates who plan to compete with their employer as part of a new venture. The circumstances of each situation must be reviewed to distinguish permissible preparations from violations of duty. Activities that might constitute a violation, especially in combination, include the following:

- misappropriation of trade secrets,
- misuse of confidential information,
- solicitation of employer's clients prior to cessation of employment,
- self-dealing (appropriating for one's own property a business opportunity or information belonging to one's employer),
- misappropriation of clients or client lists.

A departing employee is generally free to make arrangements or preparations to go into a competitive business before terminating the relationship with his or her employer provided that such preparations do not breach the employee's duty of loyalty. However, members and candidates contemplating seeking other employment must not contact existing clients or potential clients prior to leaving their employer for purposes of soliciting their business for the new employer. In addition, they must not take records or files to a new employer without the written permission of the previous employer.

Once an employee has left the firm, the skills and experience that an employee obtains while employed are not "confidential" or "privileged" information. Similarly, simple knowledge of the names and existence of former clients is generally not confidential information unless deemed such by an agreement or by law. Standard IV(A) does not impose a prohibition on the use of experience or knowledge gained at one employer from being used at another employer. However, firm records or work performed on behalf of the firm stored on a home computer for the member or candidate's convenience while employed should be erased or returned to the employer unless the firm gives permission to keep those records after employment ends.

Nor does the standard prohibit former employees from contacting clients of their previous firm so long as the contact information does not come from the records of the former employer or violate an applicable non-compete agreement. Members and candidates are free to use public information about their former firm after departing to contact former clients without violating Standard IV(A), absent a specific agreement not to do so.

Employers often require employees to sign "non-compete" agreements that preclude a departing employee from engaging in certain conduct. Members and candidates should take care to review the terms of any such agreements when leaving their employer to determine what, if any, conduct those agreements may prohibit.

Whistleblowing. A member or candidate's personal interests, as well as the interests of his or her employer, are secondary to protecting the integrity of capital markets and the interests of the clients. Therefore, there may be circumstances in which members and candidates act contrary to their employer interests in an effort to comply with their duties to the market and clients (e.g., when an employer is engaged in illegal or unethical activity). In such instances, activities that would normally violate a member or candidate's duty to his or her employer (such as contradicting employer instructions, violating certain policies and procedures, or preserving a record by copying employer records) may be justified. Such action would be permitted only if the intent is clearly aimed at protecting clients or the integrity of the market and not for personal gain.

Nature of Employment. A wide variety of business relationships exist within the investment industry. For instance, a member or candidate can be retained as an employee or independent contractor. Members and candidates must determine whether they are employees or independent contractors in order to determine the applicability of Standard IV(A). This issue will be decided largely by the degree of control exercised by the employing entity over the member or candidate. Factors determining control include whether the member or candidate's hours, work location, and other parameters of the job are set; whether facilities are provided to the member or candidate; whether the member or candidate's expenses are reimbursed; whether the member or candidate holds himself or herself out to other employers for additional work; and the number of clients or employers the member or candidate works for.

A member or candidate's duties within an independent contractor relationship are governed by the oral or written agreement between the member and the client. Members and candidates should take care to define clearly the scope of their responsibilities and the expectations of each client within the context of each relationship. Once the member or candidate establishes a relationship with a client, they have a duty to abide by the terms of the agreement.

Applications

Example 1. Samuel Magee manages pension accounts for Trust Assets, Inc., but has become frustrated with the working environment and has been offered a position with Fiduciary Management. Before resigning from Trust Assets, Magee asks four big accounts to leave that firm and open accounts with Fiduciary. Magee also persuades several prospective clients to sign agreements with Fiduciary Management. Magee had previously made presentations to these prospects on behalf of Trust Assets, Inc.

> *Comment*: Magee violated the employee–employer principle requiring him to act solely for his employer's benefit. Magee's duty is to Trust Assets as long as he is employed there. The solicitation of Trust Assets' current clients and prospective clients is unethical and violates Standard IV(A).

Example 2. James Hightower has been employed by Jason Investment Management Corporation for 15 years. He began as an analyst but assumed increasing responsibilities and is now a senior portfolio manager and a member of the firm's investment policy committee. Hightower has decided to leave Jason Investment and start his own investment management business. He has been careful not to tell any of Jason's clients that he is leaving, because he does not want to be accused of breaching his duty to Jason by soliciting Jason's clients before his departure. Hightower is planning to copy and take with him the following documents and information he developed or worked on while at Jason: (1) the client list, with addresses, telephone numbers, and other pertinent client information; (2) client account statements; (3) sample marketing presentations to prospective clients containing Jason's performance record; (4) Jason's recommended list of securities; (5) computer models to determine asset allocations for accounts with different objectives; (6) computer models for stock selection; and (7) personal computer spreadsheets for Hightower's major corporate recommendations which he developed when he was an analyst.

> *Comment*: Except with the consent of their employer, departing employees may not take employer property, which includes books, records, reports, and other materials, and may not interfere with their employer's business opportunities. Taking any employer records, even those the member or candidate prepared, violates Standard IV(A).

Example 3. Rueben Winston manages all-equity portfolios at Target Asset Management (TAM), a large, established investment counselor. Ten years ago, Philpott & Company, which manages a family of global bond mutual funds, acquired TAM in a diversification move. After the merger, the combined operations prospered in the fixed-income business while the equity management business at TAM languished. Lately, a few of the equity pension accounts that had been with TAM before the merger have terminated their relationships with TAM. One day, Winston finds on his voice mail a message from a concerned client, "Hey! I just heard that Philpott is close to announcing the sale of your firm's equity management business to Rugged Life. What is going on?" Not being aware of any such deal, Winston and his associates are stunned. Their internal inquiries are met with denials from Philpott management, but the rumors persist. Feeling left in the dark, Winston contemplates leading an employee buyout of TAM's equity management business.

Comment: An employee-led buyout of TAM's equity asset management business would be consistent with Standard IV(A) because it would rest on the permission of the employer and, ultimately, the clients. In this case, however, in which employees suspect the senior managers or principals are not truthful or forthcoming, members should consult legal counsel to determine appropriate action.

Example 4. Laura Clay, who is unemployed, wants part-time consulting work while seeking a full-time analyst position. During an interview at Bradley Associates, a large institutional asset manager, Clay is told that the firm has no immediate research openings but would be willing to pay her a flat fee to complete a study of the wireless communications industry within a given period of time. Clay would be allowed unlimited access to Bradley's research files and would be welcome to come to the offices and use whatever support facilities are available during normal working hours. Bradley's research director does not seek any exclusivity for Clay's output, and the two agree to the arrangement on a handshake. As Clay nears completion of the study, she is offered an analyst job in the research department of Winston & Company, a brokerage firm, and she is pondering submitting the draft of her wireless study for publication by Winston.

Comment: Although she is under no written contractual obligation to Bradley, Clay has an obligation to let Bradley act on the output of her study before Winston & Company or Clay uses the information to its own advantage. That is, unless Phere gives permission to Clay waiving rights to her wireless report, Clay would be in violation of Standard IV(A) if she were to immediately recommend to Winston the same transactions recommended in the report to Bradley. Furthermore, Clay must not take from Bradley any research file material or other property that she may have used.

Example 5. Emma Madeline, a recent college graduate and a candidate in the CFA Program, spends her summer as an unpaid intern at Murdoch and Lowell. Murdoch and Lowell is attempting to bring the firm into compliance with the GIPS standards, and Madeline is assigned to assist in its efforts. Two months into her internship, Madeline applies for a job at McMillan & Company, which has plans to become GIPS compliant. Madeline accepts the job with McMillan. Before leaving Murdoch, she copies the firm's software that she helped develop, as she believes this software will assist her in her new position.

Comment: Even though Madeline does not receive monetary compensation for her services at Murdoch, she has used firm resources in creating the software and she is considered an employee because she receives compensation and benefits in the form of work experience and knowledge. By copying the software, Madeline violated Standard IV(A) because she misappropriated Murdoch's property without permission.

Example 6. Dennis Elliot has hired Sam Chisolm who previously worked for a competing firm. Chisolm left his former firm after 18 years of employment. When Chisolm begins working for Elliot, he wants to contact his former clients because he knows them well and is certain that many will follow him to his new employer. Is Chisolm in violation of the standard IV(A) if he contacts his former clients?

> *Comment:* Because client records are the property of the firm, contacting former clients for any reason through the use of client lists or other information taken from a former employer without permission would be a violation of Standard IV(A). In addition, the nature and extent of the contact with former clients may be governed by the terms of any non-compete agreement signed by the employee and the former employer that covers contact with former clients after employment.
>
> But, simple knowledge of the names and existence of former clients is not confidential information, just as skills or experience that an employee obtains while employed is not "confidential" or "privileged" information. The Code and Standards do not impose a prohibition on the use of experience or knowledge gained at one employer from being used at another employer. The Code and Standards also do not prohibit former employees from contacting clients of their previous firm, absent a non-compete agreement. Members and candidates are free to use public information about their former firm after departing to contact former clients without violating Standard IV(A).
>
> In the absence of a non-compete agreement, as long as Chisolm maintains his duty of loyalty to his employer before joining Elliots' firm, does not take steps to solicit clients until he has left his former firm, and does not make use of material from his former employer without its permission after he has left, he would not be in violation of the Code and Standards.

Example 7. Gardner Allen currently works at a registered investment company as an equity analyst. Without notice to her employer, she registers with government authorities to start an investment company that will compete with her employer. However, she has not actively sought clients. Does registration of this competing company with the appropriate regulatory authorities constitute a violation of IV(A)?

> *Comment:* Allen's preparations for the new business by registering with the regulatory authorities do not conflict with the work for her employer if the preparations have been done on Allen's own time outside of the office and if Allen will not be getting clients for the business or otherwise operating the new company until she has left her current employer.

Example 8. Several employees are planning to depart their current employer within a few weeks and have been careful to not engage in any activities that would conflict with their duty to their current employer. They have just learned that one of their employer's clients has undertaken a request for proposal (RFP) to review and possibly hire a new investment consultant. The RFP has been sent to the employer and all of its competitors. The group believes that the new entity to be formed would be qualified to respond to the RFP and eligible for the business. The RFP submission period is likely to conclude before the employees' resignations are effective. Is it permissible for the group of departing employees to respond to the RFP under their anticipated new firm?

> *Comment*: A group of employees responding to an RFP that their employer is also responding to would lead to direct competition between the employees and the employer. Such conduct would violate Standard IV(A) unless the group of employees received permission from their employer as well as the entity sending out the RFP.

Example 9. Alfonso Mota is a research analyst with Tyson Investments. He works part time as a mayor for his hometown, a position for which he receives compensation. Must Mota seek permission from Tyson to serve as mayor?

> *Comment*: If Mota's mayoral duties are so extensive and time consuming that they might detract from his ability to fulfill his responsibilities at Tyson, he should discuss his outside activities with his employer and come to a mutual agreement regarding how to manage his personal commitments with his responsibilities to his employer.

Example 10. After leaving her employer, Shawna McQuillen establishes her own money management business. While with her former employer, she did not sign a "non-compete" agreement that would have prevented her from soliciting former clients. Upon her departure, she does not take any of her client lists or contact information and clears her personal computer of any employer records, including client contact information. She obtains the phone numbers of her former clients through public records and contacts them to solicit their business.

> *Comment*: McQuillen is not in violation of Standard IV(A) because she has not used information or records from her former employer and is not prevented by an agreement with her former employer from soliciting her former clients.

Standard IV: Duties to Employers

(B) Additional Compensation Arrangements

Members and Candidates must not accept gifts, benefits, compensation, or consideration that competes with, or might reasonably be expected to create a conflict of interest with, their employer's interest unless they obtain written consent from all parties involved.

Guidance

Standard IV(B) requires members and candidates to obtain permission from their employer before accepting compensation or other benefits from third parties for the services rendered to the employer or for any services that might create a conflict of interest with their employer's interest. Compensation and benefits include direct compensation by the client and any indirect compensation or other benefits received from third parties. "Written Consent" includes any form of communication that can be documented (for example, communication via computer e-mail that can be retrieved and documented).

Members and candidates must obtain permission for additional compensation/benefits because such arrangements may affect loyalties and objectivity and create potential conflicts of interest. Disclosure allows an employer to consider the outside arrangements when evaluating the actions and motivations of members and candidates. Moreover, the employer is entitled to have full knowledge of compensation/benefit arrangements to assess the true cost of the services members or candidates are providing.

Recommended Procedures for Compliance

Members and candidates should make an immediate written report to their employer specifying any compensation they propose to receive for services in addition to the compensation or benefits received from their employer. This written report should state the terms of any agreement under which a member or candidate will receive additional compensation; terms include the nature of the compensation, the approximate amount of compensation, and the duration of the agreement.

Applications

Example 1. Geoff Whitman, a portfolio analyst for Adams Trust Company, manages the account of Carol Cochran, a client. Whitman is paid a salary by his employer, and Cochran pays the trust company a standard fee based on the market value of assets in her portfolio. Cochran proposes to Whitman that "any year that my portfolio achieves at least a 15 percent return before taxes, you and your wife can fly to Monaco at my expense and use my condominium during the third week of January." Whitman does not inform his employer of the arrangement and vacations in Monaco the following January as Cochran's guest.

> *Comment:* Whitman violated Standard IV(B) by failing to inform his employer in writing of this supplemental, contingent compensation arrangement. The nature of the arrangement could have resulted in partiality to Cochran's account, which could have detracted from Whitman's performance with respect to other accounts he handles for Adams Trust. Whitman must obtain the consent of his employer to accept such a supplemental benefit.

Example 2. Terry Jones sits on the board of directors of Exercise Unlimited, Inc. In return for his services on the board, Jones receives unlimited membership privileges for his family at all Exercise Unlimited facilities. Jones purchases Exercise Unlimited stock for the client accounts for which it is appropriate. Jones does not disclose this arrangement to his employer, as he does not receive monetary compensation for his services to the board.

> *Comment:* Jones violated Standard IV(B) by failing to disclose to his employer benefits received in exchange for his services on the board of directors.

Standard IV: Duties to Employers

(C) Responsibilities of Supervisors

Members and Candidates must make reasonable efforts to detect and prevent violations of applicable laws, rules, regulations, and the Code and Standards by anyone subject to their supervision or authority.

Guidance

Standard IV(C) states that members and candidates must take steps to prevent persons acting under their supervision from violating the law, rules, regulations, or the Code and Standards.

Any investment professionals who have employees subject to their control or influence—whether or not the employees are CFA Institute members, CFA charterholders, or candidates in the CFA Program—exercise supervisory responsibility. Members and candidates acting as supervisors must have in-depth knowledge of the Code and Standards and must apply this knowledge in discharging their supervisory responsibilities.

The conduct that constitutes reasonable supervision in a particular case depends on the number of employees supervised and the work performed by those employees. Members and candidates who supervise large numbers of employees cannot personally evaluate the conduct of their employees on a continuing basis. Although these members and candidates may delegate supervisory duties, such delegation does not relieve them of their supervisory responsibility. Their responsibilities under Standard IV(C) include instructing those subordinates to whom supervision is delegated regarding methods to prevent and detect violations.

Members and candidates with supervisory responsibility must make reasonable efforts to detect violations of laws, rules, regulations, and the Code and Standards. They exercise reasonable supervision by establishing and implementing written compliance procedures and ensuring that those procedures are followed through periodic review. If a member or candidate has adopted reasonable procedures and taken steps to institute an effective compliance program, then the member or candidate may not be in violation of Standard IV(C) if they do not detect violations that occur despite these efforts. The fact that violations do occur may indicate, however, that the compliance procedures are inadequate. In addition, in some cases, merely enacting such procedures may not be sufficient to fulfill the duty required by Standard IV(C). A member or candidate may be in violation of Standard IV(C) if he or she knows or should know that the procedures designed to detect and prevent violations are not being followed.

Compliance Procedures. Members and candidates with supervisory responsibility also must understand what constitutes an adequate compliance system for their firms and make reasonable efforts to see that appropriate compliance procedures are established, documented, communicated to covered personnel, and followed. "Adequate" procedures are those designed to meet industry standards, regulatory requirements, the requirements of the Code and Standards, and the circumstances of the firm. Once compliance procedures are established, the supervisor must also make reasonable efforts to ensure that the procedures are monitored and enforced.

To be effective, compliance procedures must be in place prior to the occurrence of a violation of the law or the Code and Standards. Although compliance procedures cannot be designed to anticipate every potential violation, they should be designed to anticipate the activities most likely to result in misconduct. Each compliance program must be appropriate for the size and nature of the organization. Model compliance procedures or other industry programs should be reviewed to ensure that procedures meet the minimum industry standards.

A member or candidate with supervisory responsibility should bring an inadequate compliance system to the attention of the firm's senior managers and recommend corrective action. If the member or candidate clearly cannot discharge supervisory responsibilities because of the absence of a compliance system or because of an inadequate compliance system, the member or candidate should decline in writing to accept supervisory responsibility until the firm adopts reasonable procedures to allow them to adequately exercise such responsibility.

Once a supervisor learns that an employee has violated or may have violated the law or the Code and Standards, the supervisor must promptly initiate an investigation to ascertain the extent of the wrongdoing. Relying on an employee's statements about the extent of the violation or assurances that the wrongdoing will not reoccur is not enough. Reporting the misconduct up the chain of command and warning the employee to cease the activity are also not enough. Pending the outcome of the investigation, a supervisor should take steps to ensure the violations will not be repeated, such as placing limits on the employee's activities or increasing the monitoring of the employee's activities.

Recommended Procedures for Compliance

Members and candidates are encouraged to recommend that their employers adopt a code of ethics. Adoption of a code of ethics is critical to establishing a strong ethical foundation for investment adviser firms and their employees. Codes of ethics formally emphasize and reinforce the fiduciary responsibilities of investment firm personnel, protect investing clients by deterring misconduct, and protect the firm's reputation for integrity.

There is a distinction between codes of ethics and the necessary specific policies and procedures needed to ensure compliance with the code of conduct and securities laws and regulations. While both are important, codes of ethics should consist of fundamental, principle-based ethical and fiduciary concepts that are applicable to all of the firm's employees. In this way, firms can best convey to employees and clients the ethical ideals that investment advisers strive to achieve. These concepts can then be implemented by detailed, firmwide compliance policies and procedures. Compliance procedures will assist the firm's personnel in fulfilling the responsibilities enumerated in the code of ethics and ensure that the ideals expressed in the code of ethics are adhered to in the day-to-day operation of the firm.

Commingling compliance procedures in the firm's code of ethics will diminish the goal of reinforcing with the firm's employees their ethical obligations. Stand-alone codes of ethics should be written in plain language and address general fiduciary concepts, unencumbered by numerous detailed procedures directed to the day-to-day operation of the firm. In this way, codes will be most effective in stressing to employees that they are in positions of trust and must act with integrity at all times.

Separating the codes of ethics from compliance procedures will also reduce, if not eliminate, the legal terminology and boilerplate language that can make the underlying ethical principles incomprehensible to the average person. Above all, the principles in the codes of ethics must be accessible and understandable to everyone in the firm to ensure that a culture of ethics and integrity is created rather than merely a focus on attention to the rules.

In addition, members and candidates should encourage their employers to provide their codes of ethics to clients. But only simple, straightforward codes of ethics will be understandable to clients and thus be effective in conveying the message that the firm is committed to conducting business in an ethical manner and in the best interests of the clients.

A supervisor complies with Standard IV(C) by identifying situations in which legal violations or violations of the Code and Standards are likely to occur and by establishing and enforcing compliance procedures to prevent such violations. Adequate compliance procedures should:

- be contained in a clearly written and accessible manual that is tailored to the member or candidate's operations;
- be drafted so that the procedures are easy to understand;
- designate a compliance officer whose authority and responsibility are clearly defined and who has the necessary resources and authority to implement the firm's compliance procedures;
- describe the hierarchy of supervision and assign duties among supervisors;
- implement a system of checks and balances;
- outline the scope of the procedures;

- outline procedures to document the monitoring and testing of compliance procedures;
- outline permissible conduct;
- delineate procedures for reporting violations and sanctions.

Once a compliance program is in place, a supervisor should:

- disseminate the contents of the program to appropriate personnel;
- periodically update procedures to ensure that the measures are adequate under the law;
- continually educate personnel regarding the compliance procedures;
- issue periodic reminders of the procedures to appropriate personnel;
- incorporate a professional conduct evaluation as part of an employee's performance review;
- review the actions of employees to ensure compliance and identify violators;
- take the necessary steps to enforce the procedures once a violation has occurred.

Once a violation is discovered, a supervisor should:

- respond promptly;
- conduct a thorough investigation of the activities to determine the scope of the wrongdoing;
- increase supervision or place appropriate limitations on the wrongdoer pending the outcome of the investigation.

Applications

Example 1. Jane Mattock, senior vice president and head of the research department of H&V, Inc., a regional brokerage firm, has decided to change her recommendation for Timber Products from buy to sell. In line with H&V's procedures, she orally advises certain other H&V executives of her proposed actions before the report is prepared for publication. As a result of his conversation with Mattock, Dieter Frampton, one of the executives of H&V accountable to Mattock, immediately sells Timber's stock from his own account and from certain discretionary client accounts. In addition, other personnel inform certain institutional customers of the changed recommendation before it is printed and disseminated to all H&V customers who have received previous Timber reports.

> *Comment:* Mattock failed to supervise reasonably and adequately the actions of those accountable to her. She did not prevent or establish reasonable procedures designed to prevent dissemination of or trading on the information by those who knew of her changed recommendation. She must ensure that her firm has procedures for reviewing or recording trading in the stock of any corporation that has been the subject of an unpublished change in recommendation. Adequate procedures would have informed the subordinates of their duties and detected sales by Frampton and selected customers.

Example 2. Deion Miller is the research director for Jamestown Investment Programs. The portfolio managers have become critical of Miller and his staff because the Jamestown portfolios do not include any stock that has been the subject of a merger or tender offer. Georgia Ginn, a member of Miller's staff, tells Miller that she has been studying a local company, Excelsior, Inc., and recommends its purchase. Ginn adds that the company has been widely rumored to be the subject of a merger study by a well-known conglomerate and discussions between them are under way. At Miller's request, Ginn prepares a memo recommending the stock. Miller passes along Ginn's memo to the portfolio managers prior to leaving for vacation, noting that he has not reviewed the memo. As a result of the memo, the portfolio managers buy Excelsior stock immediately. The day Miller returns to the office, Miller learns that Ginn's only sources for the report were her brother, who is an acquisitions analyst with Acme Industries and the "well-known conglomerate" and that the merger discussions were planned but not held.

> *Comment:* Miller violated Standard IV(C) by not exercising reasonable supervision when he disseminated the memo without checking to ensure that Ginn had a reasonable and adequate basis for her recommendations and that Ginn was not relying on material nonpublic information.

Example 3. David Edwards, a trainee trader at Wheeler & Company, a major national brokerage firm, assists a customer in paying for the securities of Highland, Inc., by using anticipated profits from the immediate sale of the same securities. Despite the fact that Highland is not on Wheeler's recommended list, a large volume of its stock is traded through Wheeler in this manner. Roberta Ann Mason is a Wheeler vice president responsible for supervising compliance with the securities laws in the trading department. Part of her compensation from Wheeler is based on commission revenues from the trading department. Although she notices the increased trading activity, she does nothing to investigate or halt it.

> *Comment:* Mason's failure to adequately review and investigate purchase orders in Highland stock executed by Edwards and her failure to supervise the trainee's activities violated Standard IV(C). Supervisors should be especially sensitive to actual or potential conflicts between their own self-interests and their supervisory responsibilities.

Example 4. Samantha Tabbing is senior vice president and portfolio manager for Crozet, Inc., a registered investment advisory and registered broker/dealer firm. She reports to Charles Henry, the president of Crozet. Crozet serves as the investment advisor and principal underwriter for ABC and XYZ public mutual funds. The two funds' prospectuses allow Crozet to trade financial futures for the funds for the limited purpose of hedging against market risks. Henry, extremely impressed with Tabbing's performance in the past two years, directs Tabbing to act as portfolio manager for the funds. For the benefit of its employees, Crozet has also organized the Crozet Employee Profit-Sharing Plan (CEPSP), a defined-contribution retirement plan. Henry assigns Tabbing to manage 20 percent of the assets of CEPSP. Tabbing's investment objective for her portion of CEPSP's assets is aggressive growth. Unbeknownst to Henry, Tabbing frequently places S&P 500 Index purchase and sale orders for the funds and the CEPSP without providing the futures commission merchants (FCMs) who take the orders with any prior or simultaneous designation of the account for which the trade has been placed. Frequently, neither Tabbing nor anyone else at Crozet completes an internal trade ticket to record the time an order was placed or the specific account for which the order was intended. FCMs often designate a specific account only after the trade, when Tabbing provides such designation. Crozet has no written operating procedures or compliance manual concerning its futures trading, and its compliance department does not review such trading. After observing the market's movement, Tabbing assigns to CEPSP the S&P 500 positions with more-favorable execution prices and assigns positions with less-favorable execution prices to the funds.

> *Comment*: Henry violated Standard IV(C) by failing to adequately supervise Tabbing with respect to her S&P 500 trading. Henry further violated Standard IV(C) by failing to establish record-keeping and reporting procedures to prevent or detect Tabbing's violations.

Standard V: Investment Analysis, Recommendations, and Actions

---

(A) Diligence and Reasonable Basis

Members and Candidates must:

1. Exercise diligence, independence, and thoroughness in analyzing investments, making investment recommendations, and taking investment actions.

2. Have a reasonable and adequate basis, supported by appropriate research and investigation, for any investment analysis, recommendation, or action.

Guidance

The application of Standard V(A) is dependent on the investment philosophy followed, the role of the member or candidate in the investment decision-making process, and the support and resources provided by the member or candidate's employer. These factors will dictate the nature of the diligence, thoroughness of the research, and level of investigation required by Standard V(A).

The requirements for issuing conclusions on research will vary based on the member or candidate's role in the investment decision-making process, but the member or candidate must make reasonable efforts to cover all pertinent issues when arriving at the recommendation. Members and candidates enhance transparency by providing or offering to provide supporting information to clients when recommending a purchase or sale or when changing a recommendation.

Using Secondary or Third-Party Research. If members and candidates rely on secondary or third-party research, they must make reasonable and diligent efforts to determine whether such research is sound. Secondary research is defined as research conducted by someone else in the member or candidate's firm. Third-party research is research conducted by entities outside the member or candidate's firm, such as a brokerage firm, bank, or research firm. If a member or candidate has reason to suspect that either secondary or third-party research or information comes from a source that lacks a sound basis, the member or candidate must refrain from relying on that information. This requirement also applies in situations involving quantitatively oriented research, such as computer-generated screening or ranking of universes of equity securities based on various sets of prescribed criteria. Examples of criteria that a member or candidate can use in forming his or her opinion that research is sound include:

- review of the assumptions used,
- rigor of analysis performed,
- date/timeliness of the research, and
- evaluation of the objectivity and independence of recommendations.

When a member or candidate relies on others within his or her firm to determine whether secondary or third-party research is sound, the information can be used in good faith unless the member or candidate has reason to question its validity or the processes and procedures used by those responsible for the investigation. An example of this situation would be a portfolio manager who does not have a choice over a data source because the firm's senior management conducted due diligence to determine which vendor would provide services.

Group Research and Decision Making. Commonly, members and candidates may be part of a group or team that is collectively responsible for producing investment analysis or research. The conclusions or recommendations of the report represent the consensus of the group and are not necessarily the views of the member or candidate, even though the name of the member or candidate is included on the report. There may be many instances when the member or candidate does not agree with the independent and objective view of the group. If the member or candidate believes that consensus opinion has a reasonable and adequate basis, then the member or candidate does not necessarily have to decline to be identified with the report. There should be a presumption that the group members are independent and objective and have a reasonable basis for the opinions. If the member or candidate is confident in the process, the member or candidate does not have to dissociate from the report if it does not reflect his or her opinion. The member or candidate should, however, document his or her difference of opinion with the team.

Recommended Procedures for Compliance

Members and candidates should encourage their firms to consider the following policies and procedures to support the principles of Standard V(A):

- Establish a policy requiring that research reports and recommendations have a basis that can be substantiated as reasonable and adequate. An individual employee (supervisory analyst) or a group of employees (review committee) should be appointed to review and approve all research reports and recommendations prior to external circulation to determine whether they meet the criteria as established in the policy.
- Develop detailed, written guidance for research analysts, supervisory analysts, and review committees that establishes due-diligence procedures for judging whether a particular recommendation has a reasonable and adequate basis.
- Develop measurable criteria for assessing the quality of research, including the reasonableness and adequacy of the basis for any recommendation and the accuracy of recommendations over time, and implement compensation arrangements that depend on these measurable criteria and that are applied consistently to all research analysts.

Application of the Standard

Example 1. Helen Hawke manages the corporate finance department of Sarkozi Securities, Ltd. The firm is anticipating that the government will soon close a tax loophole that currently allows oil and gas exploration companies to pass on drilling expenses to holders of a certain class of shares. Because market demand for this tax-advantaged class of stock is currently high, Sarkozi convinces several companies to undertake new equity financings at once before the loophole closes. Time is of the essence, but Sarkozi lacks sufficient resources to conduct adequate research on all the prospective issuing companies. Hawke decides to estimate the IPO prices based on the relative size of each company and to justify the pricing later when her staff has time.

> *Comment:* Sarkozi should have taken on only the work that it could adequately handle. By categorizing the issuers as to general size, Hawke has bypassed researching all the other relevant aspects that should be considered when pricing new issues and thus has not performed sufficient due diligence. Such an omission can result in investors purchasing shares at prices that have no actual basis. Hawke has violated Standard V(A).

Example 2. Babu Dhaliwal works for Heinrich Brokerage in the corporate finance group. He has just persuaded Feggans Resources, Ltd., to allow his firm to do a secondary equity financing at Feggans Resources' current stock price. Because the stock has been trading at higher multiples than similar companies with equivalent production, Dhaliwal presses the Feggans Resources managers to project what would be the maximum production they could achieve in an optimal scenario. Based on these numbers, he is able to justify the price his firm will be asking for the secondary issue. During a sales pitch to the brokers, Dhaliwal then uses these numbers as the base-case production levels that Feggans Resources will achieve.

> *Comment:* When presenting information to the brokers, Dhaliwal should have given a range of production scenarios and the probability of Feggans Resources achieving each level. By giving the maximum production level as the likely level of production, he has misrepresented the chances of achieving that production level and seriously misled the brokers.

Example 3. Brendan Witt creates an Internet site with a chat-room area to publish his stock recommendations. He views the site as a chance to attract new clients. In the chat room, he almost always writes positively about technology stocks and recommends purchasing based on what the conventional wisdom of the markets has deemed the "hot" securities of the day.

Comment: Witt's exuberance about technology and the conventional wisdom of the markets, without more information, do not constitute a reasonable and adequate basis, supported by appropriate research and investigation, on which to base a recommendation. Therefore, Witt has violated Standard V(A).

Example 4. Carsten Dunlop is an investment consultant in the London office of EFG, a major global investment consultant firm. One of her U.K. pension funds has decided to appoint a specialist U.S. equity manager. EFG's global manager research relies on local consultants to cover managers within their region and, after conducting thorough due diligence, post their views and ratings on EFG's manager database. Dunlop accesses EFG's global manager research database and conducts a screen of all U.S. equity managers based on the client's desired match for philosophy/style, performance, and tracking-error targets and those that are rated "buy." She selects the five managers meeting these criteria and puts them in a briefing report that is delivered to the client 10 days later. In between the time of Dunlop's database search and delivery of the report to the client, EFG updated the database with the information that one of the firms that Dunlop has recommended for consideration lost its chief investment officer, head of U.S. equity research, and the majority of portfolio managers on the U.S. equity product—all of whom have left to establish their own firm, and she does not provide the client with this updated information. Although EFG has updated its database, Dunlop's report to the client does not reflect this new information.

Comment: Dunlop has failed to satisfy the requirement of Standard V(A) by not checking the database in a timely manner and updating her report to the client. Although EFG updated the manager ratings to reflect the personnel turnover at the firm, Dunlop did not update her report to reflect the new information.

Example 5. Evelyn Mastakis is a junior analyst asked by her firm to write a research report predicting the expected interest rate for residential mortgages over the next six months. Mastakis submits her report to the fixed-income investment committee of her firm for review, as required by firm procedures. Although some committee members support Mastakis's conclusion, the majority of the committee disagrees with her conclusion and the report is significantly changed to indicate that interest rates are likely to increase more than originally predicted by Mastakis.

Comment: The results of research are not always clear, and different people may have different opinions based on the same factual evidence. In this case, the majority of the committee may have valid reasons for issuing a report that differs from the analyst's original research. The firm can issue a report different from the original report of the analyst as long as there is a reasonable or adequate basis for its conclusions. Generally, analysts must write research reports that reflect their own opinion and can ask the firm not to put their name on reports that ultimately differ from that opinion. When the work is a group effort, however, not all members of the team may agree with all aspects of the report. Ultimately, members and candidates can ask to have their names removed from the report, but if they are satisfied that the process has produced results or conclusions that have a reasonable or adequate basis, members or candidates do not have to dissociate from the report even when they do not agree with its contents. The member or candidate should document the difference of opinion and any request to remove his or her name from the report.

Example 6. Gary McDermott runs a small, two-person investment management firm. McDermott's firm subscribes to a service from a large investment research firm that provides research reports. McDermott's firm makes investment recommendations based on these reports.

> *Comment:* Members and candidates can rely on third-party research but must make reasonable and diligent efforts to determine that such research is sound. If McDermott undertakes due diligence efforts on a regular basis to ensure that the research produced by the large firm is objective and reasonably based, McDermott can rely on that research when making investment recommendations to clients.

Standard V: Investment Analysis, Recommendations, and Actions

(B) Communication with Clients and Prospective Clients

Members and Candidates must:

1. Disclose to clients and prospective clients the basic format and general principles of the investment processes used to analyze investments, select securities, and construct portfolios and must promptly disclose any changes that might materially affect those processes.

2. Use reasonable judgment in identifying which factors are important to their investment analyses, recommendations, or actions and include those factors in communications with clients and prospective clients.

3. Distinguish between fact and opinion in the presentation of investment analysis and recommendations.

Guidance

Standard V(B) addresses member and candidate conduct with respect to communicating with clients. Developing and maintaining clear, frequent, and thorough communication practices is critical to providing high-quality financial services to clients. When clients can understand the information communicated to them, they also can understand exactly how members and candidates are acting on their behalf, which gives clients the opportunity to make well-informed decisions regarding their investments. Such understanding can be accomplished only through clear communication.

Standard V(B) states the responsibility of members and candidates to include in their communications those key factors that are instrumental to the investment recommendation presented. A critical part of this requirement is to distinguish clearly between opinions and facts. In preparing a research report, the member or candidate must present the basic characteristics of the security being analyzed, which will allow the reader to evaluate the report and incorporate information the reader deems relevant to his or her investment decision-making process.

Members and candidates must adequately illustrate to clients and prospective clients the manner in which the member or candidate conducts the investment decision-making process. The member or candidate must keep existing clients and other interested parties informed with respect to changes to the chosen investment process on an ongoing basis. Only by thoroughly understanding the nature of the investment product or service can a client determine whether changes to that product or service could materially affect the client's investment objectives.

Understanding the basic characteristics of the investment is of great importance in judging the suitability of each investment on a stand-alone basis, but it is especially important in determining the impact each investment will have on the characteristics of the portfolio. For instance, although the risk and return characteristics of shares of a common stock might seem to be essentially the same for any investor when the stock is viewed in isolation, the implications of such an investment vary greatly depending on the other investments held. If the particular stock represents 90 percent of an individual's investments, the stock's importance in the portfolio is vastly different from what it would be to an investor who holds the same amount of the stock in a highly diversified portfolio in which the stock represents only 2 percent of the holdings.

For purposes of Standard V(B), communication is not confined to a written report of the type traditionally generated by an analyst researching a particular security, company, or industry. A presentation of information can be made via any means of communication, including in-person recommendation, telephone conversation, media broadcast, or transmission by computer (e.g., on the Internet). Furthermore, the nature of these communications is highly diverse—from one word ("buy" or "sell") to in-depth reports of more than 100 pages. Brief communications must be supported by background reports or data that can be made available to interested parties on request.

A communication may contain a general recommendation about the market, asset allocation, or classes of investments (e.g., stocks, bonds, real estate) or relate to a specific security. If recommendations are contained in capsule form (such as a recommended stock list), members and candidates should notify clients that additional information and analyses are available from the producer of the report. Investment advice based on quantitative research and analysis must be supported by readily available reference material and should be applied in a manner consistent with previously applied methodology or with changes in methodology highlighted. Members and candidates should outline known limitations of the analysis and conclusions contained in their investment analysis. In evaluating the basic characteristics of the investment being recommended, members and candidates should consider in the report the principal risks inherent in the expected cash returns, which may include credit risk, financial risk (specifically the use of leverage or financial derivatives), and overall market risk.

Once the process has been completed, the member or candidate who prepares the report must include those elements important to the analysis and conclusions of the report so that the user can follow and challenge the report's reasoning. A report writer who has done adequate investigation may emphasize certain areas, touch briefly on others, and omit certain aspects deemed unimportant. For instance, a report may dwell on a quarterly earnings release or new-product introduction at the sacrifice of examining other fundamental matters in depth so long as the analyst clearly stipulates the limits to the scope of the report.

Standard V(B) requires that opinion be separated from fact. Violations are most likely to occur when reports fail to separate the past from the future by not indicating that earnings estimates, changes in the outlook for dividends, and/or future market price information are opinions subject to future circumstances. In the case of complex quantitative analysis, analysts must clearly separate fact from statistical conjecture and should identify the known limitations of the analysis.

Recommended Procedures for Compliance

Because the selection of relevant factors is an analytical skill, determination of whether a member or candidate has used reasonable judgment in excluding and including information in research reports depends heavily on case-by-case review rather than a specific checklist. To assist in the after-the-fact review of a report, the member or candidate must maintain records indicating the nature of the research and should, if asked, be able to supply additional information to the client (or any user of the report) covering factors not included.

Application of the Standard

Example 1. Sarah Williamson, director of marketing for Country Technicians, Inc., is convinced that she has found the perfect formula for increasing Country Technician's income and diversifying its product base. Williamson plans to build on Country Technician's reputation as a leading money manager by marketing an exclusive and expensive investment advice letter to high-net-worth individuals. One hitch in the plan is the complexity of Country Technician's investment system—a combination of technical trading rules (based on historical price and volume fluctuations) and portfolio-construction rules designed to minimize risk. To simplify the newsletter, she decides to include only each week's top-five buy and sell recommendations and to leave out details of the valuation models and the portfolio-structuring scheme.

> *Comment:* Williamson's plans for the newsletter violate Standard V(B) because she does not intend to include all the relevant factors behind the investment advice. Williamson need not describe the investment system in detail in order to implement the advice effectively, clients must be informed of Country Technician's basic process and logic. Without understanding the basis for a recommendation, clients cannot possibly understand its limitations or its inherent risks.

Example 2. Richard Dox is a mining analyst for East Bank Securities. He has just finished his report on Boisy Bay Minerals. Included in his report is his own assessment of the geological extent of mineral reserves likely to be found on the company's land. Dox completed this calculation based on the core samples from the company's latest drilling. According to Dox's calculations, the company has in excess of 500,000 ounces of gold on the property. Dox concludes his research report as follows: "Based on the fact that the company has 500,000 ounces of gold to be mined, I recommend a strong BUY."

> *Comment*: If Dox issues the report as written, he will violate Standard V(B). His calculation of the total gold reserves for the property is an opinion, not a fact. Opinion must be distinguished from fact in research reports.

Example 3. Olivia Thomas, an analyst at Government Brokers, Inc., which is a brokerage firm specializing in government bond trading, has produced a report that describes an investment strategy designed to benefit from an expected decline in U.S. interest rates. The firm's derivative products group has designed a structured product that will allow the firm's clients to benefit from this strategy. Thomas's report describing the strategy indicates that high returns are possible if various scenarios for declining interest rates are assumed. Citing the proprietary nature of the structured product underlying the strategy, the report does not describe in detail how the firm is able to offer such returns in the scenarios, nor does the report address the likely returns of the strategy if, contrary to expectations, interest rates rise.

> *Comment*: Thomas has violated Standard V(B) because her report fails to describe properly the basic characteristics of the investment strategy, including how the structure was created and the degree to which leverage was embedded in the structure. The report should include a balanced discussion of how the strategy would perform in the case of rising as well as falling interest rates.

Example 4. May & Associates is an aggressive growth manager that has represented itself since its inception as a specialist at investing in small-capitalization domestic stocks. One of May's selection criteria is a maximum capitalization of $250 million for any given company. After a string of successful years of superior relative performance, May expanded its client base significantly, to the point at which assets under management now exceed $3 billion. For liquidity purposes, May's chief investment officer (CIO) decides to lift the maximum permissible market-cap ceiling to $500 million and change the firm's sales and marketing literature accordingly to inform prospective clients and third-party consultants.

> *Comment*: Although May's CIO is correct about informing potentially interested parties as to the change in investment process, he must also notify May's existing clients. Among the latter group might be a number of clients who not only retained May as a small-cap manager but also retained mid-cap and large-cap specialists in a multiple-manager approach. Such clients could regard May's change of criteria as a style change that could distort their overall asset allocations.

Example 5. Rather than lifting the ceiling for its universe from $250 million to $500 million, May & Associates extends its small-cap universe to include a number of non-U.S. companies.

> *Comment:* Standard V(B) requires that May's CIO advise May's clients of this change because the firm may have been retained by some clients specifically for its prowess at investing in domestic small-cap stocks. Other variations requiring client notification include introducing derivatives to emulate a certain market sector or relaxing various other constraints, such as portfolio beta. In all such cases, members and candidates must disclose changes to all interested parties.

Example 6. RJZ Capital Management is a value-style active equity manager that selects stocks using a combination of four multifactor models. Because of favorable results gained from back-testing the most recent 10 years of available market data, the president of RJZ decides to replace its simple model of price to trailing 12-months earnings with a new dividend discount model designed by the firm that is a function of projected inflation rates, earnings growth rates, and interest rates.

> *Comment:* Because the introduction of a new and different valuation model represents a material change in the investment process, RJZ's president must communicate the change to the firm's clients. RJZ is moving away from a model based on hard data toward a new model that is at least partly dependent on the firm's forecasting skills. Clients would likely view such a model as a significant change rather than a mere refinement of RJZ's process.

Example 7. RJZ Capital Management loses the chief architect of its multifactor valuation system. Without informing its clients, the president of RJZ decides to redirect the firm's talents and resources toward developing a product for passive equity management–a product that will emulate the performance of a major market index.

> *Comment:* The president of RJZ failed to disclose to clients a substantial change to its investment process, which is a violation of Standard V(B).

Example 8. At Fundamental Asset Management, Inc., the responsibility for selecting stocks for addition to the firm's "approved" list has just shifted from individual security analysts to a committee consisting of the research director and three senior portfolio managers. Eleanor Morales, a portfolio manager with Fundamental Asset Management, fails to notify her clients of the change.

> *Comment:* Morales must disclose the process change to all her clients. Some of Fundamental's clients might be concerned about the morale and motivation among the firm's best research analysts following the change. Moreover, clients might challenge the stock-picking track record of the portfolio managers and might even want to monitor the situation closely.

Standard V: Investment Analysis, Recommendations, and Actions

(C) Record Retention

Members and Candidates must develop and maintain appropriate records to support their investment analysis, recommendations, actions, and other investment-related communications with clients and prospective clients.

Guidance

Members and candidates must retain records that substantiate the scope of their research and reasons for their actions or conclusions. The records required to support recommendations and/or investment actions depend on the role of the member or candidate in the investment decision-making process. Records can be maintained either in hard copy or electronic form.

As a general matter, records created as part of a member or candidate's professional activity on behalf of his or her employer are the property of the member or candidate's firm. When a member or candidate leaves a firm to seek other employment, the member or candidate cannot take the property of the firm, including originals or copies of supporting records of the member or candidate's work, to the new employer without the express consent of the previous employer. Without re-creating the records at the new firm, the member or candidate cannot use historical recommendations or research reports created at the previous firm because the supporting documentation is unavailable.

Local regulators often impose requirements on members, candidates, and their firms related to record retention that must be followed. Fulfilling such regulatory requirements also may satisfy the requirements of Standard V(C), but members and candidates should explicitly determine whether it does. In the absence of regulatory guidance, CFA Institute recommends maintaining records for at least seven years.

Recommended Procedures for Compliance

The responsibility to maintain records that support investment action generally falls with the firm rather than individuals. However, members and candidates must retain research notes and other documents supporting current investment-related communications to assist their firms in complying with internal or external record preservation requirements.

Application of the Standard

Example 1. One of Nikolas Lindstrom's clients is upset by the negative investment returns in his equity portfolio. The investment policy statement for the client requires that the portfolio manager follow a benchmark-oriented approach. The benchmark for the client included a 35 percent investment allocation in the technology sector, which the client acknowledged was appropriate. Over the past three years, the portion put into the segment of technology stocks suffered severe losses. The client complains to the investment manager that so much money was allocated to this sector.

> *Comment*: For Lindstrom, it is important to have appropriate records to show that over the past three years the percentage of technology stocks in the benchmark index was 35 percent. Therefore, the amount of money invested in the technology sector was appropriate according to the investment policy statement. Lindstrom should also have the investment policy statement for the client stating that the benchmark was appropriate for the client's investment objectives. He should also have records indicating that the investment had been explained appropriately to the client and that the investment policy statement was updated on a regular basis.

Example 2. Malcolm Young is a research analyst who writes numerous reports rating companies in the luxury retail industry. His reports are based on a variety of sources, including interviews with company management, manufacturers, and economists; onsite company visits; customer surveys; and secondary research from analysts covering related industries.

> *Comment*: Young must carefully document and keep copies of all the information that goes into his report, including the secondary or third-party research of other analysts.

Example 3. Martin Blank develops an analytical model while employed by Grosse Point Investment Management, LLP (GPIM). While at the firm, he systematically documents the assumptions that make up the model as well has his reasoning for the assumptions. As the result of the success of his model, Blank is hired to be the head of the research department of one of GPIM's competitors. Blank takes copies of the records supporting his model to his new firm.

> *Comment*: The records created by Blank supporting the research model he developed at GPIM are the records of GPIM. He cannot take the documents with him to his new employer without GPIM's permission [see Standard III(A)]. Blank must re-create the records supporting his model at the new firm.

Standard VI: Conflicts of Interest

(A) Disclosure of Conflicts

Members and Candidates must make full and fair disclosure of all matters that could reasonably be expected to impair their independence and objectivity or interfere with respective duties to their clients, prospective clients, and their employer. Members and Candidates must ensure that such disclosures are prominent, are delivered in plain language, and communicate the relevant information effectively.

Guidance

Conflicts of interest often arise in the investment management profession. Conflicts can occur between the interests of clients, the interests of employers, and the member or candidate's own personal interest. Managing these conflicts is a critical part of working in the investment industry and can take many forms. Best practice is to avoid conflicts of interest when possible. When conflicts cannot be reasonably avoided, disclosure of their existence is necessary.

Standard VI(A) protects investors and employers by requiring members and candidates to fully disclose to clients, potential clients, and employers all actual and potential conflicts of interest. Once a member or candidate has made full disclosure, the member or candidate's employer, clients, and prospects will have the information needed to evaluate the objectivity of the investment advice or action taken on their behalf.

To be effective, disclosures must be prominent and must be made in plain language and in a manner designed to effectively communicate the information to clients and prospective clients. It is up to members and candidates to determine how often, in what manner, or under what particular circumstances disclosure of conflicts must be made. Members and candidates have the responsibility to assess when and how they meet their obligations under this standard in each particular case. Members and candidates should err on the side of caution or repetition to ensure that conflicts of interest are effectively communicated.

Disclosure to Clients. Members and candidates must maintain their objectivity when rendering investment advice or taking investment action. Investment advice or actions may be perceived to be tainted in numerous situations. Can a member or candidate remain objective if, on behalf of the firm, the member or candidate obtains or assists in obtaining fees for services? Can a member or candidate give objective advice if he or she owns stock in the company that is the subject of an investment recommendation or if the member or candidate has a close personal relationship with the company managers? Requiring members and candidates to disclose all matters that reasonably could be expected to impair the member or candidate's objectivity allows clients and prospects to judge motives and possible biases for themselves.

In the investment industry, a conflict, or the perception of a conflict, often cannot be avoided. The most obvious conflicts of interest, which should always be disclosed, are relationships between the member, candidate, or their firm and an issuer (such as a directorship or consultancy), investment banking, underwriting and financial relationships, broker/dealer market-making activities, and material beneficial ownership of stock. A member or candidate must take reasonable steps to determine if a conflict of interest exists and disclose to clients any conflicts of the member or candidate's firm when known. Disclosure of broker/dealer market-making activities alerts clients that a purchase or sale might be made from or to the firm's principal account and that the firm has a special interest in the price of the stock.

Service as a director poses three basic conflicts of interest. First, a conflict may exist between the duties owed to clients and the duties owed to shareholders of the company. Second, investment personnel who serve as directors may receive the securities or the option to purchase securities of the company as compensation for serving on the board, which could raise questions about trading actions that could increase the value of those securities. Third, board service creates the opportunity to receive material non-public information involving the company. Even though the information is confidential, the perception could be that information not available to the public might be communicated to a director's firm—whether a broker, investment advisor, or other type of organization. When members or candidates providing investment services also serve as directors, they should be isolated from those making investment decisions by the use of fire walls or similar restrictions.

Many other circumstances give rise to actual or potential conflicts of interest. For instance, a sell-side analyst working for a broker/dealer may be encouraged, not only by members of her or his own firm but by corporate issuers themselves, to write research reports about particular companies. The buy-side analyst is likely to be faced with similar conflicts as banks exercise their underwriting and securities-dealing powers. The marketing division may ask an analyst to recommend the stock of a certain company in order to obtain business from that company.

The potential for conflicts of interest also exists with broker-sponsored limited partnerships formed to invest venture capital. Increasingly, members and candidates are expected not only to follow issues from these partnerships once they are offered to the public but also to promote the issues in the secondary market after public offerings. Members, candidates, and their firms should attempt to resolve situations presenting potential conflicts of interest or disclose them in accordance with the principles set forth in Standard VI(A).

The most prevalent conflict requiring disclosure under Standard VI(A) is a member or candidate's ownership of stock in companies that they recommend to clients and/or that clients hold. Clearly, the easiest method for preventing a conflict is to prohibit members and candidates from owning any such securities, but this approach is over burdensome and discriminates against members and candidates.

Therefore, sell-side members and candidates should disclose any materially beneficial ownership interest in a security or other investment that the member or candidate is recommending. Buy-side members and candidates should disclose their procedures for reporting requirements for personal transactions. For the purposes of Standard VI(A), members and candidates beneficially own securities or other investments if they have a direct or indirect pecuniary interest in the securities; have the power to vote or direct the voting of the shares of the securities or investments; or have the power to dispose or direct the disposition of the security or investment. Conflicts arising from personal investing are discussed more fully in the guidance for Standard VI(B).

Disclosure of Conflicts to Employers. Disclosure of conflicts to employers may also be appropriate in many instances. When reporting conflicts of interest to employers, members and candidates should give their employer enough information to assess the impact of the conflict. By complying with employer guidelines, members and candidates allow their employers to avoid potentially embarrassing and costly ethical or regulatory violations.

Reportable situations include conflicts that would interfere with rendering unbiased investment advice and conflicts that would cause a member or candidate not to act in the employer's best interest. The same circumstances that generate conflicts to be reported to clients and prospects also would dictate reporting to employers. Ownership of stocks analyzed or recommended, participation in outside boards, and financial and other pressures that may influence a decision are to be promptly reported to the employer so that their impact can be assessed and a decision made on how to resolve the conflict.

The mere appearance of conflict of interest may create problems for members, candidates, and their employers. Therefore, many of the conflicts previously mentioned could be explicitly prohibited by the employer. For example, many employers restrict personal trading, outside board membership, and related activities to prevent situations that might not normally be considered problematic from a conflict-of-interest point of view but that could give the appearance of a conflict of interest. Members and candidates must comply with these restrictions. Members and candidates must take reasonable steps to avoid conflicts and, if they occur inadvertently, must report them promptly so that the employer and the member or candidate can resolve them as quickly and effectively as possible.

Standard VI(A) also deals with a member or candidate's conflicts of interest that might be detrimental to the employer's business. Any potential conflict situation that could prevent clear judgment in or full commitment to the execution of the member or candidate's duties to the employer should be reported to the member or candidate's employer and promptly resolved.

Recommended Procedures for Compliance

Members or candidates should disclose special compensation arrangements with the employer that might conflict with client interests, such as bonuses based on short-term performance criteria, commissions, incentive fees, performance fees, and referral fees. If the member or candidate's firm does not permit such disclosure, the member or candidate should document the request and may consider dissociating from the activity.

Members or candidates' firms are encouraged to include information on compensation packages in firms' promotional literature. If a member or candidate manages a portfolio for which the fee is based on a share of capital gains or capital appreciation (a performance fee), this information should be disclosed to clients. If a member, candidate, or a member or candidate's firm has outstanding agent options to buy stock as part of the compensation package for corporate financing activities, the amount and expiration date of these options should be disclosed as a footnote to any research report published by the member or candidate's firm.

Applications

Example 1. Hunter Weiss is a research analyst with Farmington Company, a broker and investment banking firm. Farmington's merger and acquisition department has represented Vimco, a conglomerate, in all of its acquisitions for 20 years. From time to time, Farmington officers sit on the boards of directors of various Vimco subsidiaries. Weiss is writing a research report on Vimco.

> *Comment*: Weiss must disclose in his research report Farmington's special relationship with Vimco. Broker/dealer management of and participation in public offerings must be disclosed in research reports. Because the position of underwriter to a company presents a special past and potential future relationship with a company that is the subject of investment advice, it threatens the independence and objectivity of the report and must be disclosed.

Example 2: The investment management firm of Dover & Roe sells a 25 percent interest in its partnership to a multinational bank holding company, First of New York. Immediately thereafter, Margaret Hobbs, president of Dover & Roe, changes her recommendation of First of New York's common stock from "sell" to "buy" and adds First of New York's commercial paper to Dover & Roe's approved list for purchase.

> *Comment*: Hobbs must disclose the new relationship with First of New York to all Dover & Roe clients. This relationship must also be disclosed to clients by the firm's portfolio managers when they make specific investment recommendations or take investment actions with respect to First of New York's securities.

Example 3. Carl Fargmon, a research analyst who follows firms producing office equipment, has been recommending purchase of Kincaid Printing because of its innovative new line of copiers. After his initial report on the company, Fargmon's wife inherits from a distant relative $3 million of Kincaid stock. He has been asked to write a follow-up report on Kincaid.

> *Comment*: Fargmon must disclose his wife's ownership of the Kincaid stock to his employer and in his follow-up report. Best practice would be to avoid the conflict by asking his employer to assign another analyst to draft the follow-up report.

Example 4. Betty Roberts is speculating in penny stocks for her own account and purchases 100,000 shares of Drew Mining, Inc., for 30 cents a share. She intends to sell these shares at the sign of any substantial upward price movement of the stock. A week later, her employer asks her to write a report on penny stocks in the mining industry to be published in two weeks. Even without owning the Drew stock, Roberts would recommend it in her report as a "buy." A surge of the price of the stock to the $2 range is likely to result once the report is issued.

> *Comment*: Although this holding may not be material, Roberts must disclose it in the report and to her employer before writing the report because the gain for her will be substantial if the market responds strongly to her recommendation. The fact that she has only recently purchased the stock adds to the appearance that she is not entirely objective.

Example 5. Samantha Dyson, a portfolio manager for Thomas Investment Counsel, Inc., specializes in managing defined-benefit pension plan accounts, all of which are in the accumulative phase and have long-term investment objectives. A year ago, Dyson's employer, in an attempt to motivate and retain key investment professionals, introduced a bonus compensation system that rewards portfolio managers on the basis of quarterly performance relative to their peers and certain benchmark indexes. Dyson changes her investment strategy and purchases several high-beta stocks for client portfolios in an attempt to improve short-term performance. These purchases are seemingly contrary to the client investment policy statement. Now, an officer of Griffin Corporation, one of Dyson's pension fund clients, asks why Griffin Corporation's portfolio seems to be dominated by high-beta stocks of companies that often appear among the most actively traded issues. No change in objective or strategy has been recommended by Dyson during the year.

> *Comment*: Dyson violated Standard VI(A) by failing to inform her clients of the changes in her compensation arrangement with her employer that created a conflict of interest. Firms may pay employees on the basis of performance, but pressure by Thomas Investment Counsel to achieve short-term performance goals is in basic conflict with the objectives of Dyson's accounts.

Example 6. Wayland Securities works with small companies doing IPOs and/or secondary offerings. Typically, these deals are in the $10 million to $50 million range and, as a result, the corporate finance fees are quite small. In order to compensate for the small fees, Wayland Securities usually takes "agents options"– that is, rights (exercisable within a two-year time frame) to acquire up to an additional 10 percent of the current offering. Following an IPO performed by Wayland for Falk Resources, Ltd., Darcy Hunter, the head of corporate finance at Wayland, is concerned about receiving value for her Falk Resources options. The options are one month from expiring, and the stock is not doing well. She contacts John Fitzpatrick in the research department of Wayland Securities, reminds him that he is eligible for 30 percent of these options, and indicates that now would be a good time to give some additional coverage to Falk Resources. Fitzpatrick agrees and immediately issues a favorable report.

> *Comment:* In order for Fitzpatrick not to be in violation of Standard VI(A), he must indicate in the report the volume and expiration date of agent options outstanding. Furthermore, because he is personally eligible for some of the options, Fitzpatrick must disclose the extent of this compensation. He also must be careful that he does not violate his duty of independence and objectivity under Standard I(B).

Example 7. Gary Carter is a representative with Bengal International, a registered broker/dealer. Carter is approached by a stock promoter for Badger Company, who offers to pay Carter additional compensation for sales to his clients of Badger Company's stock. Carter accepts the stock promoter's offer but does not disclose the arrangements to his clients or to his employer. Carter sells shares of the stock to his clients.

> *Comment:* Carter has violated Standard VI(A) by failing to disclose to clients that he was receiving additional compensation for recommending and selling Badger stock. Because he did not disclose the arrangement with Badger to his clients, the clients were unable to evaluate whether Carter's recommendations to buy Badger were affected by this arrangement. Carter's conduct also violated Standard VI(A) by failing to disclose to his employer monetary compensation received in addition to the compensation and benefits conferred by his employer. Carter was required by Standard VI(A) to disclose the arrangement with Badger to his employer so that his employer could evaluate whether the arrangement affected his objectivity and loyalty.

Example 8. Carol Corky, a senior portfolio manager for Universal Management, recently became involved as a trustee with the Chelsea Foundation, a very large not-for-profit foundation in her hometown. Universal is a small money manager (with assets under management of approximately $100 million) that caters to individual investors. Chelsea has assets in excess of $2 billion. Corky does not believe informing Universal of her involvement with Chelsea is necessary.

Comment: By failing to inform Universal of her involvement with Chelsea, Corky violated Standard VI(A). Given the large size of the endowment at Chelsea, Corky's new role as a trustee can reasonably be expected to be time consuming, to the possible detriment of Corky's portfolio responsibilities with Universal. As a trustee, Corky also may become involved with the investment decisions at Chelsea. Therefore, Standard VI(A) obligates Corky to discuss becoming a trustee at Chelsea with her compliance officer or supervisor at Universal before accepting the position and she should have disclosed the degree to which she would be involved in investment decisions at Chelsea.

Example 9. Bruce Smith covers East European equities for Marlborough investments, an investment management firm with a strong presence in emerging markets. While on a business trip to Russia, Smith learns that investing in Russian equity directly is difficult but that equity-linked notes that replicate the performance of the underlying Russian equity can be purchased from a New York-based investment bank. Believing that his firm would not be interested in such a security, Smith purchases a note linked to a Russian telecommunications company for his own account without informing Marlborough. A month later, Smith decides that the firm should consider investing in Russian equities using equity-linked notes, and he prepares a write-up on the market that concludes with a recommendation to purchase several of the notes. One note recommended is linked to the same Russian telecom company that Smith holds in his personal account.

Comment: Smith violated Standard VI(A) by failing to disclose his ownership of the note linked to the Russian telecom company. Smith is required by the standard to disclose the investment opportunity to his employer and look to his company's policies on personal trading to determine whether it was proper for him to purchase the note for his own account. By purchasing the note, Smith may or may not have impaired his ability to make an unbiased and objective assessment of the appropriateness of the derivative instrument for his firm, but Smith's failure to disclose the purchase to his employer impaired his employer's ability to render an opinion regarding whether the ownership of the security constituted a conflict of interest that might have affected future recommendations. Once he recommended the notes to his firm, Smith compounded his problems by not disclosing that he owned the notes in his personal account–a clear conflict of interest.

Standard VI: Conflicts of Interest

> ## (B) Priority of Transactions
>
> Investment transactions for clients and employers must have priority over investment transactions in which a Member or Candidate is the beneficial owner.

Guidance

Standard VI(B) reinforces the responsibility of members and candidates to give the interests of their clients and employers priority over their personal financial interests. This standard is designed to prevent any potential conflict of interest or the appearance of a conflict of interest with respect to personal transactions. Client interests have priority. Client transactions must take precedence over transactions made on behalf of the member or candidate's firm or personal transactions.

Standard VI(B) states that transactions for clients and employers must have priority over transactions in securities or other investments of which a member or candidate is the beneficial owner so that such personal transactions do not adversely affect the interests of their clients or employers. For purposes of the Code and Standards, a member or candidate is a "beneficial owner" if the member or candidate has a direct or indirect personal interest in the securities. A member or candidate having the same investment positions or being co-invested with their clients does not always create a conflict. Some clients in certain investment situations require members or candidates to have aligned interests. However, personal investment positions or transactions of a member or candidate or their firm should never adversely affect client investments.

Conflicts between the client's interest and an investment professional's personal interest may occur. Although conflicts of interest exist, there is nothing inherently unethical about individual managers, advisors, or mutual fund employees making money from personal investments as long as (1) the client is not disadvantaged by the trade, (2) the investment professional does not benefit personally from trades undertaken for clients, and (3) the investment professional complies with applicable regulatory requirements.

Standard VI(B) covers the activities of all members and candidates who have knowledge of pending transactions that may be made on behalf of their clients or employers. Standard VI(B) also applies to members and candidates who have access to information during the normal preparation of research recommendations or who take investment actions. Members and candidates are prohibited from conveying such information to any person whose relationship to the member or candidate makes the member or candidate a beneficial owner of the person's securities. Members and candidates must not convey this information to any other person if the information can be deemed material nonpublic information.

Members or candidates may undertake transactions in accounts for which they are a beneficial owner only after their clients and employers have had adequate opportunity to act on the recommendation. Personal transactions include those made for the member or candidate's own account, for family (including spouse, children, and other immediate family members) accounts, and for accounts in which the member or candidate has a direct or indirect pecuniary interest, such as a trust or retirement account. Family accounts that are client accounts should be treated like any other firm account and should neither be given special treatment nor be disadvantaged because of an existing family relationship with the member or candidate. If a member or candidate has a beneficial ownership in the account, however, the member or candidate may still be subject to pre-clearance or reporting requirements of their employer or applicable law.

Recommended Procedures for Compliance

Policies and procedures designed to prevent potential conflicts of interest, or even the appearance of a conflict of interest, with respect to personal transactions are critical to establishing investor confidence in the securities industry. Because investment firms vary greatly in assets under management, types of clients, number of employees, and so on, each firm should establish policies regarding personal investing that are best suited to the firm. Members and candidates should then prominently disclose those policies to clients and prospective clients.

The specific provisions of each firm's standards will vary, but all firms should adopt certain basic procedures to address the conflict areas created by personal investing. These include:

Limited participation in equity IPOs. Some eagerly awaited IPOs may significantly rise in value shortly after the issue is brought to market. Because the new issue may be highly attractive and sought after, the opportunity to participate in the IPO may be limited. Therefore, purchases of IPOs by investment personnel create conflicts of interest in two principal ways. First, participation in an IPO may have the appearance of appropriating an attractive investment opportunity from clients for personal gain—a clear breach of the duty of loyalty to clients. Second, because opportunities to participate in IPOs are limited, there may be an appearance that the investment opportunity is being bestowed as an incentive to make future investment decisions for the benefit of the party providing the opportunity. Members and candidates can avoid these conflicts or the appearance of a conflict of interest by not participating in IPOs.

Reliable and systematic review procedures should be established to ensure that conflicts relating to IPOs are identified and appropriately dealt with by supervisors. Members and candidates should preclear their participation in IPOs, even in situations were there are no conflicts of interest between a member or candidate's participation in an IPO and the client's interests. Members and candidates should not benefit from the position that their clients occupy in the marketplace—through preferred trading, the allocation of limited offerings, and/or oversubscription.

Restrictions on private placements. Strict limits should be placed on investment personnel acquiring securities in private placements, and appropriate supervisory and review procedures should be established to prevent noncompliance.

Firms do not routinely use private placements for clients (e.g., venture capital deals) because of the high risk associated with them. Conflicts relating to private placements are more significant to members and candidates who manage large pools of assets or act as plan sponsors because these managers may be offered special opportunities, such as private placements, as a reward or an enticement for continuing to do business with a particular broker.

Participation in private placements raises conflict-of-interest issues that are similar to issues surrounding IPOs. Investment personnel should not be involved in transactions, including (but not limited to) private placements that could be perceived as favors or gifts that seem designed to influence future judgment or to reward past business deals.

Whether the venture eventually proves to be good or bad, managers have an immediate conflict concerning private placement opportunities. Participants in private placements have an incentive to recommend these investments to clients if and when they go public, regardless of the suitability of the investments for their clients, in order to increase the value of the participants' personal portfolios.

Establish blackout/restricted periods. Investment personnel involved in the investment decision-making process should establish blackout periods prior to trades for clients so that managers cannot take advantage of their knowledge of client activity by "front-running" client trades.

Individual firms must decide who within the firm should be required to comply with the trading restrictions. At a minimum, all individuals who are involved in the investment decision-making process should be subject to the same restricted period. Each firm must determine specific requirements relating to blackout and restricted periods that are most relevant to the firm while ensuring that the procedures are governed by the guiding principles set forth in the Code and Standards. Size of firm and type of securities purchased are relevant factors. For example, in a large firm, a blackout requirement is, in effect, a total trading ban because the firm is continually trading in most securities. In a small firm, the blackout period is more likely to prevent the investment manager from front-running.

Reporting requirements. Supervisors should establish reporting procedures for investment personnel, including duplicate confirmations, disclosure of personal holdings/beneficial ownerships, and preclearance procedures. Once trading restrictions are in place, they must be enforced. The best method for monitoring and enforcing procedures established to eliminate conflicts of interest relating to personal trading is through reporting requirements, including the following:

- Disclosure of holdings in which the employee has a beneficial interest. Disclosure by investment personnel to the firm should be made upon commencement of the employment relationship and at least annually thereafter. To address privacy considerations, disclosure of personal holdings should be handled in a confidential manner by the firm.

- Providing duplicate confirmations of transactions. Investment personnel should be required to direct their brokers to supply duplicate copies or confirmations to their firms of all their personal securities transactions and copies of periodic statements for all securities accounts. Firms should establish additional reporting requirements, including the frequency of such reporting, that emphasize the firm's intention to promote full and complete disclosure and that explain the role and responsibilities of supervisors. The duplicate confirmation requirement has two purposes: (1) The requirement sends a message that "people are looking" and makes it difficult for an individual to act unethically, and (2) it enables verification of the accounting of the flow of personal investments that cannot be determined from merely looking at transactions or holdings.

- Preclearance procedures. Investment personnel should clear all personal investments to identify possible conflicts prior to the execution of personal trades. Preclearance procedures are designed to identify possible conflicts before a problem arises. Preclearance procedures are consistent with the CFA Institute Code and Standards and demonstrate that members, candidates, and their firms place the interests of their clients ahead of their own personal investing interests.

Disclosure of policies. Upon request, members and candidates should fully disclose to investors their firm's personal investing policies. The infusion of information on employees' personal investment activities and policies into the marketplace will foster an atmosphere of full and complete disclosure and calm the public's legitimate concerns about the conflicts of interest posed by investment personnel's personal trading. The disclosure must be helpful to investors, however, not simply boilerplate language containing some vague admonition that investment personnel are "subject to policies and procedures regarding their personal trading."

Applications

Example 1. A research analyst, Marlon Long, does not recommend purchase of a common stock for his employer's account because he wants to purchase the stock personally and does not want to wait until the recommendation is approved and the stock purchased by his employer.

Comment: Long violated Standard VI(B) by taking advantage of his knowledge of the stock's value before allowing his employer to benefit from that information.

Example 3. Carol Baker, the portfolio manager of an aggressive-growth mutual fund, maintains an account in her husband's name at several brokerage firms with which the fund and a number of Baker's other individual clients do a substantial amount of business. Whenever a new hot issue becomes available, she instructs the brokers to buy it for her husband's account. Because such issues normally are scarce, Baker often acquires shares while her clients are not able to participate.

Comment: Baker must acquire shares for her mutual fund first and acquire them for her husband's account only after doing so, even though she might miss out on participating in new issues via her husband's account. She also must disclose the trading for her husband's account to her employer because this activity creates a conflict between her personal interests and her employer's interests [Standard VI(A)].

Example 4. Erin Toffler, a portfolio manager at Esposito Investments, manages the retirement account established with the firm by her parents. Whenever IPOs become available, she first allocates shares to all her other clients for whom the investment is appropriate; only then does she place any remaining portion in her parents' account, if the issue is appropriate for them. She has adopted this procedure so that no one can accuse her of favoring her parents.

Comment: Toffler has breached her duty to her parents by treating them differently from her other accounts simply because of the family relationship. As fee-paying clients of Esposito Investments, Toffler's parents are entitled to the same treatment as any other client of the firm. If Toffler has beneficial ownership in the account, however, and Esposito Investments has preclearance and reporting requirements for personal transactions, she may have to preclear the trades and report the transactions to Esposito.

Example 5. Gary Michaels is an entry-level employee who holds a relatively low paying job serving both the research and investment management departments of an active investment management company. He purchases a sports car and begins to wear expensive clothes after only a year of employment with the firm. The director of the investment management department, who has responsibility for monitoring the personal stock transactions of all employees, investigates and discovers that Michaels has made substantial investment gains by purchasing stocks just before they were put on the firm's recommended purchase list. Michaels was regularly given the firm's quarterly personal transaction form but declined to complete it.

Comment: Michaels violated Standard VI(B) by placing personal transactions ahead of client transactions. In addition, his supervisor violated the Standards by permitting Michaels to continue to perform his assigned tasks without first having signed the quarterly personal transaction form [Standard IV(C)]. Note also that if Michaels had communicated information about the firm's recommendations to a person who traded the security, that action would be a misappropriation of the information and a violation of Standard II(A).

Example 6. A brokerage's insurance analyst, Denise Wilson, makes a closed-circuit report to her firm's branches around the country. During the broadcast, she includes negative comments about a major company within the industry. The following day, Wilson's report is printed and distributed to the sales force and public customers. The report recommends that both short-term traders and intermediate investors take profits by selling that company's stocks. Seven minutes after the broadcast, Ellen Riley, head of the firm's trading department, closes out a long call position in the stock. Shortly thereafter, Riley establishes a sizable "put" position in the stock. Riley claims she took this action to facilitate anticipated sales by institutional clients.

Comment: Riley expected that both the stock and option markets would respond to the "sell" recommendation, but she did not give customers an opportunity to buy or sell in the options market before the firm itself did. By taking action before the report was disseminated, Riley's firm could have depressed the price of the "calls" and increased the price of the "puts." The firm could have avoided a conflict of interest if it had waited to trade for its own account until its clients had an opportunity to receive and assimilate Wilson's recommendations. As it is, Riley's actions violated Standard VI(B).

Standard VI: Conflicts of Interest

(C) Referral Fees

Members and Candidates must disclose to their employer, clients, and prospective clients, as appropriate, any compensation, consideration, or benefit received by, or paid to, others for the recommendation of products or services.

Guidance

Standard VI(C) states the responsibility of members and candidates to inform employer, clients, and prospective clients of any benefit received for referrals of customers and clients. Such disclosure will allow the client or employer to evaluate (1) any partiality shown in any recommendation of services and (2) the full cost of the services.

Appropriate disclosure means that members and candidates must advise the client or prospective client, before entry into any formal agreement for services, of any benefit given or received for the recommendation of any services provided by the member or candidate. In addition, the member or candidate must disclose the nature of the consideration or benefit—for example, flat fee or percentage basis; one-time or continuing benefit; based on performance; benefit in the form of provision of research or other noncash benefit—together with the estimated dollar value. Consideration includes all fees, whether paid in cash, in soft dollars, or in kind.

Applications

Example 1. Brady Securities, Inc., a broker/dealer, has established a referral arrangement with Lewis Brothers, Ltd., an investment counseling firm. Under this arrangement, Brady Securities refers all prospective tax-exempt accounts, including pension, profit-sharing, and endowment accounts, to Lewis Brothers. In return, Lewis Brothers makes available to Brady Securities on a regular basis the security recommendations and reports of its research staff, which registered representatives of Brady Securities use in serving customers. In addition, Lewis Brothers conducts monthly economic and market reviews for Brady Securities personnel and directs all stock commission business generated by referral accounts to Brady Securities. Willard White, a partner in Lewis Brothers, calculates that the incremental costs involved in functioning as the research department of Brady Securities amount to $20,000 annually. Referrals from Brady Securities last year resulted in fee income of $200,000, and directing all stock trades through Brady Securities resulted in additional costs to Lewis Brothers' clients of $10,000.

Diane Branch, the chief financial officer of Maxwell Inc., contacts White and says that she is seeking an investment manager for Maxwell's profit-sharing plan. She adds, "My friend Harold Hill at Brady Securities recommended your firm without qualification, and that's good enough for me. Do we have a deal?" White accepts the new account but does not disclose his firm's referral arrangement with Brady Securities.

> *Comment:* White violated Standard VI(C) by failing to inform the prospective customer of the referral fee payable in services and commissions for an indefinite period to Brady Securities. Such disclosure could have caused Branch to reassess Hill's recommendation and make a more critical evaluation of Lewis Brothers' services.

Example 2. James Handley works for the Trust Department of Central Trust Bank. He receives compensation for each referral he makes to Central Trust's brokerage and personal financial management department that results in a sale. He refers several of his clients to the personal financial management department but does not disclose the arrangement within Central Trust to his clients.

> *Comment:* Handley has violated Standard V(C) by not disclosing the referral arrangement at Central Trust Bank to his clients. The Standard does not distinguish between referral fees paid by a third party for referring clients to the third party and internal compensation arrangements paid within the firm to attract new business to a subsidiary. Members and candidates must disclose all such referral fees. Therefore, Handley would be required to disclose, at the time of referral, any referral fee agreement in place between Central Trust Bank's departments. The disclosure should include the nature and the value of the benefit and should be made in writing.

Example 3. Katherine Roberts is a portfolio manager at Katama Investments, an advisory firm specializing in managing assets for high-net-worth individuals. Katama's trading desk uses a variety of brokerage houses to execute trades on behalf of its clients. Roberts asks the trading desk to direct a large portion of its commissions to Naushon, Inc., a small broker/dealer run by one of Robert's business school classmates. Katama's traders have found that Naushon is not very competitive on pricing, and although Naushon generates some research for its trading clients, Katama's other analysts have found most of Naushon's research not especially useful. Nevertheless, the traders do as Roberts asks, and in return for receiving a large portion of Katama's business, Naushon recommends the investment services of Roberts and Katama to its wealthiest clients. This arrangement is not disclosed to either Katama or the clients referred by Naushon.

> *Comment:* Roberts violated Standard VI(C) by failing to inform her employer of the referral arrangement.

Example 4. Yeshao Wen is a portfolio manager for a bank. He receives additional monetary compensation from his employer when he is successful in assisting in the sales process and generation of assets under management. The assets in question will be invested in proprietary product offerings such as affiliate company mutual funds.

> *Comment:* Standard VI(C) is meant to address instances where the investment advice provided by a member or candidate appears to be objective and independent but in fact is influenced by an unseen referral arrangement. It is not meant to cover compensation by employers to employees for generating new business when it would be obvious to potential clients that the employees are "referring" potential clients to the services of their employers.
>
> If Wen is selling the bank's investment management services in general, he does not need to disclose to potential clients that he will receive a bonus for finding new clients and acquiring new assets under management for the bank. Potential clients are likely aware that it would be financially beneficial both to the portfolio manager and the manager's firm for the portfolio manager to sell the services of the firm and attract new clients. Therefore, sales efforts attempting to attract new investment management clients need not disclose this fact.
>
> However, in this example, the assets will be managed in "proprietary product offerings" of the manager's company (for example, an in-house mutual fund) and Wen will receive additional compensation for selling firm products. Some sophisticated investors may realize that it would be financially beneficial to the portfolio manager and the manager's firm if the investor buys the product offerings of the firm.
>
> Best practice, however, dictates that the portfolio manager must disclose to clients that they are compensated for referring clients to firm products. Such disclosure will meet the purpose of Standard VI(C), which is to allow investors to determine whether there is any partiality on the part of the portfolio manager when making investment advice.

Standard VII: Responsibilities as a CFA Institute Member or CFA Candidate

> ## (A) Conduct as Members and Candidates in the CFA Program
>
> Members and Candidates must not engage in any conduct that compromises the reputation or integrity of CFA Institute or the CFA designation or the integrity, validity, or security of the CFA examinations.

Guidance

Standard VII(A) covers the conduct of CFA Institute members and candidates involved with the CFA Program and prohibits any conduct that undermines the public's confidence that the CFA charter represents a level of achievement based on merit and ethical conduct. The standard's function is to hold members and candidates to a high ethical standard while they are participating in or involved with the CFA Program. Conduct covered includes, but is not limited to:

- cheating on the CFA examination or any other examination;
- disregarding the rules and policies of the CFA Program related to examination administration;
- providing confidential program information to candidates or the public;
- disregarding or attempting to circumvent security measures established by CFA Institute for the CFA examination;
- improperly using the CFA designation or other association with CFA Institute to further personal or professional goals; and
- misrepresenting information on the Professional Conduct Statement or the CFA Institute Professional Development Program.

This standard does not cover expressing opinions regarding the CFA Program or CFA Institute. Members and candidates are free to disagree and express their disagreement with CFA Institute on its policies, procedures, or any advocacy positions taken by the organization.

Application of the Standard

Example 1. Travis Nero serves as a proctor for the administration of the CFA examination in his city. In the course of his service, he reviews a copy of the Level II examination on the evening prior to the examination's administration and provides information concerning the examination questions to two candidates who use it to prepare for the exam.

Comment: Nero and the two candidates violated Standard VII(A). By giving information concerning the examination questions to two candidates, Nero provided an unfair advantage to the two candidates and undermined the integrity and validity of the Level II examination as an accurate measure of the knowledge, skills, and abilities necessary to earn the right to use the CFA designation. By accepting the information, the candidates also compromised the integrity and validity of the Level II examination and undermined the ethical framework that is a key part of the designation.

Example 2. Loren Sullivan is enrolled to take the Level II CFA examination. He has been having difficulty remembering a particular formula, so prior to entering the examination room, he writes the formula on the palm of his hand. During the afternoon section of the examination, a proctor notices Sullivan looking at the palm of his hand. She asks to see his hand and finds the formula to be a bit smudged but readable.

Comment: Because Sullivan wrote down information from the Candidate Body of Knowledge and took that written information into the examination, his conduct compromised the validity of his examination, and violated Standard VII(A). Sullivan's conduct was also in direct contradiction of the rules and regulations of the CFA Program, the Candidate Pledge, and the CFA Institute Code and Standards.

Example 3. Prior to participating in the CFA Examination Grading Program, Wesley Whitcomb is required to sign a CFA Institute Grader Agreement. As part of the Grader Agreement, Whitcomb agrees not to reveal or discuss the examination materials with anyone except CFA Institute staff or other graders. Several weeks after the conclusion of the CFA examination grading, Whitcomb tells several colleagues who are candidates in the CFA Program which question he graded. He also discusses the guideline answer and adds that few candidates scored well on the question.

Comment: Whitcomb violated Standard VII(A) by breaking the Grader Agreement and disclosing information related to a specific question on the examination, which compromised the integrity of the examination process.

Example 4. At the conclusion of the morning section of the Level I CFA examination, the proctors announce that all candidates are to stop writing immediately. John Davis has not completed the examination, so he continues to randomly fill in ovals on his answer sheet. A proctor approaches Davis' desk and reminds him that he should stop writing immediately; Davis, however, continues to complete the answer sheet. After the proctor asks him to stop writing two additional times, Davis finally puts down his pencil.

Comment: By continuing to complete his examination after time was called, Davis violated Standard VII(A). By continuing to write, Davis had an unfair advantage over other candidates, and his conduct compromised the validity of his examination. Additionally, by not heeding the proctor's repeated instructions, Davis violated the rules and regulations of the CFA Program.

Example 5. Ashlie Hocking is writing Level II of the CFA examination in London. After completing the exam, she immediately attempts to contact her friend in Sydney, Australia, to tip him off to specific questions on the exam.

Comment: Hocking has violated Standard VII(A) by attempting to give her friend an unfair advantage, thereby compromising the integrity of the CFA examination process.

Example 6. Jose Ramirez is an investment-relations consultant for several small companies that are seeking greater exposure to investors. He is also the program chair for the CFA Institute society in the city where he works. To the exclusion of other companies, Ramirez only schedules companies that are his clients to make presentations to the society.

Comment: Ramirez, by using his volunteer position at CFA Institute to benefit himself and his clients, compromises the reputation and integrity of CFA Institute and, thus, violates Standard VII(A).

Example 7. Marguerite Warrenski is a member of the CFA Institute Investment Performance Council (IPC), which oversees the creation, implementation, and revision of the CFA Institute performance presentation standards: the AIMR-PPS and GIPS. As a member of the IPC, she has advance knowledge of confidential information regarding both standards, including any new or revised standards the committee is considering. She tells her clients that her IPC membership will allow her to assist her clients in keeping up with changes to the standards and facilitating their compliance with the changes.

Comment: Warrenski, by using her volunteer position at CFA Institute to benefit herself and her clients, compromises the reputation and integrity of CFA Institute and, thus, violates Standard VII(A).

Standard VII: Responsibilities as a CFA Institute Member or CFA Candidate

---

(B) Reference to CFA Institute, the CFA Designation, and the CFA Program

When referring to CFA Institute, CFA Institute membership, the CFA designation, or candidacy in the CFA Program, Members and Candidates must not misrepresent or exaggerate the meaning or implications of membership in CFA Institute, holding the CFA designation, or candidacy in the CFA Program.

Guidance

Individuals may reference their CFA designation, CFA Institute membership, or candidacy in the CFA Program but must not exaggerate the meaning or implications of membership in CFA Institute, holding the CFA designation, or candidacy in the CFA Program.

This standard is intended to prevent promotional efforts that make promises or guarantees that are tied to the designation. Statements referencing CFA Institute, the CFA designation, or the CFA Program must not

- over-promise the competency of an individual or
- over-promise future investment results (e.g., higher performance, lower risk).

Statements that highlight or emphasize the commitment of CFA Institute members, CFA charterholders, and CFA candidates to ethical and professional conduct as well as the thoroughness and rigor of the CFA Program are appropriate. Members and candidates may make claims about the relative merits of CFA Institute, the CFA Program, or the Code of Ethics as long as those statements are the opinion of the speaker, whether implicitly or explicitly stated as opinion. Otherwise, statements that do not express opinion have to be supported by facts.

Standard VII(B) applies to any form of communication, including but not limited to that made in electronic or written form (such as on firm letterhead, business cards, professional biographies, directory listings, printed advertising, firm brochures, or personal resumes) and oral statements made to the public, clients, or prospects.

CFA Institute Membership. The term "CFA Institute members" refers to Regular and Affiliate members of CFA Institute who have met the membership requirements as defined in the CFA Institute Bylaws. Once accepted as a CFA Institute member, the member must satisfy the following requirements to maintain his or her status:

- remit annually to CFA Institute a completed Professional Conduct Statement, which renews the commitment to abide by the requirements of the

CFA Institute Code of Ethics and Standards of Professional Conduct and the CFA Institute Professional Conduct Program, and

- pay applicable CFA Institute membership dues on an annual basis.

If a CFA Institute member fails to meet any one of the requirements listed above, then the individual is no longer considered an active member. Until their membership is reactivated, individuals must not hold themselves out as active members. They may state, for example, that they were CFA Institute members in the past or reference the years when their membership was active.

Using the Chartered Financial Analyst Designation. Those who have earned the right to use the Chartered Financial Analyst designation may use the marks "Chartered Financial Analyst" or "CFA" and are encouraged to do so but only in a manner that does not misrepresent or exaggerate the meaning or implications of the designation. The use of the designation may be accompanied by an accurate explanation of the requirements that have been met to earn the right to use the designation.

"CFA charterholders" are those individuals who have earned the right to use the Chartered Financial Analyst designation granted by CFA Institute. These are people who have satisfied certain requirements, including completion of the CFA Program and required years of acceptable work experience. Once granted the right to use the designation, individuals must also satisfy the CFA Institute membership requirements (see above) to maintain their right to use the designation.

If a CFA charterholder fails to meet any one of the membership requirements, he or she forfeits the right to use the CFA designation. Until reactivated, individuals must not hold themselves out as CFA charterholders. They may state, for example, that they were charterholders in the past.

Referencing Candidacy in the CFA Program. Candidates in the CFA Program may reference their participation in the CFA Program, but the reference must clearly state that an individual is a candidate in the CFA Program and must not imply that the candidate has achieved any type of partial designation. A person is a candidate in the CFA Program if

- the person's application for registration in the CFA Program has been accepted by CFA Institute, as evidenced by issuance of a notice of acceptance, and the person is enrolled to sit for a specified examination; or
- the registered person has sat for a specified examination but exam results have not yet been received.

If an individual is registered for the CFA Program but declines to sit for an exam or otherwise does not meet the definition of a candidate as described in the CFA Institute Bylaws, then that individual is no longer considered an active candidate. Once the person is enrolled to sit for a future examination, his or her CFA candidacy resumes.

CFA candidates must never state or imply a partial designation for passing one or more levels or cite an expected completion date of any level of the CFA Program. Final award of the charter is subject to meeting the CFA Program requirements and approval by the CFA Institute Board.

If a candidate passes each level of the exam on the first try and wants to state that he or she did so, that is not a violation of Standard VII(B) because it is a statement of fact. If the candidate then goes on to claim or imply superior ability by obtaining the designation in only three years, he or she is in violation of Standard VII(B).

The following statements illustrate proper and improper references to the CFA designation:

Improper References

- "CFA charterholders achieve better performance results."
- "John Smith is among the elite, having passed all three CFA examinations in three consecutive attempts."
- "As a CFA charterholder, I am the most qualified to manage client investments."
- "CFA, Level II"
- "CFA, Expected 2005"

Proper References

- "Completion of the CFA Program has enhanced my portfolio management skills."
- "John Smith passed all three CFA examinations in three consecutive years."
- "The CFA designation is globally recognized and attests to a charterholder's success in a rigorous and comprehensive study program in the field of investment management and research analysis."
- "The credibility that the CFA designation affords and the skills the CFA Program cultivates are key assets for my future career development."
- "As a CFA charterholder I am committed to the highest ethical standards."
- "I enrolled in the CFA Program to obtain the highest set of credentials in the global investment management industry."
- "I passed Level I of the CFA examination."
- "I am a 2003 Level III CFA candidate."
- "I passed all three levels of the CFA Program and will be eligible for the CFA charter upon completion of the required work experience."

Proper Usage of the CFA Marks. Upon obtaining the CFA charter from CFA Institute, charterholders are given the right to use the CFA trademarks, including Chartered Financial Analyst®, CFA®, and the CFA Logo (a certification mark). These trademarks are registered by CFA Institute in countries around the world.

- The Chartered Financial Analyst and CFA marks must always be used either after a charterholder's name or as adjectives (never as nouns) in written documents or oral conversations. For example, to refer to oneself as "a CFA" or "a Chartered Financial Analyst" is improper.
- The CFA Logo certification mark is used by charterholders as a distinctive visual symbol of the CFA designation that can be easily recognized by employers, colleagues, and clients. As a certification mark, it must only be used to directly reference an individual charterholder or group of charterholders.

CFA charterholders should refer to guidelines published by CFA Institute that provide additional information and examples illustrating proper and improper use of the CFA Logo, Chartered Financial Analyst, and CFA marks. These guidelines and the CFA logo are available on the CFA Institute website at www.cfainstitute.org/memservices/cfaguide.html.

Exhibit 4. Correct and Incorrect Use of the Chartered Financial Analyst and CFA Marks

Incorrect	Principle	Correct
He is one of two CFAs in the company. He is a Chartered Financial Analyst.	The CFA and Chartered Financial Analyst designations must always be used as adjectives, never as nouns or common names.	He is one of two CFA charterholders in the company. He earned the right to use the Chartered Financial Analyst designation.
Jane Smith, C.F.A. John Doe, cfa	No periods. Always capitalize the letters "CFA"	Jane Smith, CFA
John, a CFA-type portfolio manager. The focus is on Chartered Financial Analysis. CFA equivalent program. Swiss-CFA	Do not alter the designation to create new words or phrases.	John Jones, CFA
Jones Chartered Financial Analysts, Inc.	The designation must not be used as part of the name of a firm.	John Jones, Chartered Financial Analyst
Jane Smith, **CFA** John Doe, **Chartered Financial Analyst**	The CFA designation should not be given more prominence (e.g., larger, bold) than the charterholder's name.	Jane Smith, CFA John Doe, Chartered Financial Analyst
Chartered Financial Analyst (CFA), September 2007.	Candidates in the CFA Program must not cite the expected date of exam completion and award of charter.	Level I candidate in the CFA Program.
CFA Level I. CFA degree expected in 2006.	No designation exists for someone who has passed Level I, Level II, or Level III of the exam. The CFA designation should not be referred to as a degree.	Passed Level I of the CFA examination in 2002.

Exhibit 4. Correct and Incorrect Use of the Chartered Financial Analyst and CFA Marks (continued)

Incorrect	Principle	Correct
CFA (Passed Finalist)	A candidate who has passed Level III but has not yet received his or her charter cannot use the CFA or Chartered Financial Analyst designation.	I have passed all three levels of the CFA Program and may be eligible for the CFA charter upon completion of the required work experience.
CFA, 2001, UK Society of Investment Professionals	In citing the designation in a resume, a charterholder should use the date that he or she received the designation and should cite CFA Institute as the conferring body.	CFA, 2001, CFA Institute, (optional: Charlottesville, Virginia, USA)

Recommended Procedures for Compliance

It is common for references to a member's CFA designation or CFA candidacy to be misused or improperly referenced by others within a member or candidate's firm who do not possess knowledge of the requirements of Standard VII(B). As an appropriate step to reduce this risk, members and candidates should disseminate written information on Standard VII(B) and the accompanying guidance to their firm's legal, compliance, public relations, and marketing departments. Information on proper use of the designation can be found on the CFA Institute website at www.cfainstitute.org/memservices/pdf/trademark_usage.pdf. For materials that reference employees' affiliation with CFA Institute, members and candidates should encourage their firms to create templates that are approved by a central authority (such as the compliance department) as being consistent with Standard VII(B). This practice would promote consistency and accuracy of references to CFA Institute membership, the CFA designation, and CFA candidacy within the firm.

Application of the Standard

Example 1. An advertisement for AZ Investment Advisors states that all the firm's principals are CFA charterholders and all passed the three examinations on their first attempt. The advertisement prominently links this fact to the notion that AZ's mutual funds have achieved superior performance.

> *Comment:* AZ may state that all principals passed the three examinations on the first try as long as this statement is true and is not linked to performance or does not imply superior ability. Implying that (1) CFA charterholders achieve better investment results and (2) those who pass the exams on the first try may be more successful than those who do not violates Standard VII(B).

Example 2. Five years after receiving his CFA charter, Louis Vasseur resigns his position as an investment analyst and spends the next two years traveling abroad. Because he is not actively engaged in the investment profession, he does not file a completed Professional Conduct Statement with CFA Institute and does not pay his CFA Institute membership dues. At the conclusion of his travels, Vasseur becomes a self-employed analyst, accepting assignments as an independent contractor. Without reinstating his CFA Institute membership by filing his Professional Conduct Statement and paying his dues, he prints business cards that display "CFA" after his name.

> *Comment*: Vasseur has violated Standard VII(B) because Vasseur's right to use the CFA designation was suspended when he failed to file his Professional Conduct Statement and stopped paying dues. Therefore, he no longer is able to state or imply that he is an active CFA charterholder. When Vasseur files his Professional Conduct Statement and resumes paying CFA Institute dues to activate his membership, he will be eligible to use the CFA designation upon satisfactory completion of CFA Institute reinstatement procedures.

Example 3. After a 25-year career, James Simpson retires from his firm. Because he is not actively engaged in the investment profession, he does not file a completed Professional Conduct Statement with CFA Institute and does not pay his CFA Institute membership dues. Simpson designs a plain business card (without a corporate logo) to hand out to friends with his new contact details, and he continues to put "CFA" after his name.

> *Comment*: Simpson has violated Standard VII(B). If he wants to obtain "retired" status in terms of his CFA Institute membership and CFA charter status, he needs to file the appropriate paperwork with CFA Institute to be recognized as such. By failing to file his Professional Conduct Statement and ceasing to pay dues, his membership is suspended and he gives up his right to use the CFA designation. When Simpson receives his notification from CFA Institute that his membership has been reclassified as "retired" and he resumes paying reduced dues, his membership will be reactivated and his right to use the CFA designation will be reinstated.

Example 4. Asia Futures Ltd is a small quantitative investment advisory firm. The firm takes great pride in the fact that all its employees are CFA charterholders. To underscore this fact, the firm's senior partner is proposing to change the firm's letterhead to include the following:

Asia Futures Ltd.

Comment: The CFA Logo is a certification mark intended to identify individual charterholders and must not be incorporated into a company name, confused with a company logo, or placed in such close proximity to a company name or logo as to give the reader the idea that the certification mark certifies the company. It would only be appropriate to use the CFA Logo on the business card or letterhead of each individual CFA charterholder.

Example 5. Rhonda Reese has been a CFA charterholder since 2000. In a conversation with a friend who is considering enrolling in the CFA Program, she states that she has learned a great deal from the CFA Program and that many firms require their employees to be CFA charterholders. She would recommend the CFA Program to anyone pursuing a career in investment management.

Comment: Reese's comments comply with Standard VII(B). Her statements refer to enhanced knowledge and the fact that many firms require the CFA designation for their investment professionals.

Example 6. Tatiana Prittima has earned both her CFA designation and a PhD in finance. She would like to cite both her accomplishments on her business card but is unsure of the proper method for doing so.

Comment: The order of designations cited on such items as resumes and business cards is a matter of personal preference. Prittima is free to cite the CFA designation either before or after listing her PhD.

CFA INSTITUTE Standards of Practice Exam
(with Answers and Analysis)

Standards of Practice Examination

Unless otherwise stated in the question, all individuals in the following questions are CFA Institute members or candidates in the CFA program and, therefore, are subject to the CFA Institute Code of Ethics and Standards of Professional Conduct.

1. Smith, a research analyst with a brokerage firm, decides to change his recommendation on the common stock of Green Company, Inc., from a buy to a sell. He mails this change in investment advice to all the firm's clients on Wednesday. The day after the mailing, a client calls with a buy order for 500 shares of Green Company. In this circumstance, Smith should:

    a. Accept the order.
    b. Advise the customer of the change in recommendation before accepting the order.
    c. Not accept the order until five days have elapsed after the communication of the change in recommendation.
    d. Not accept the order because it is contrary to the firm's recommendation.

2. All of the following statements about a manager's use of clients' brokerage commissions are true *except*:

    a. Clients may direct a manager to use that client's brokerage commissions to purchase goods and services for that client.
    b. Client brokerage commissions may be used by the manager to pay for securities research used in managing the client's portfolio.
    c. Client brokerage commissions should be used to benefit the client and should be commensurate with the value of the brokerage and research services received.
    d. Client brokerage commissions may be directed to pay for the investment manager's operating expenses.

3. Jamison is a junior research analyst with Howard & Howard, a brokerage and investment banking firm. Howard & Howard's mergers and acquisitions department has represented the Britland Company in all of its acquisitions for the past 20 years. Two of Howard & Howard's senior officers are directors of various Britland subsidiaries. Jamison has been asked to write a research report on Britland. What is the best course of action for her to follow?

    a. Jamison may write the report but must refrain from expressing any opinions because of the special relationships between the two companies.
    b. Jamison may write the report so long as the officers agree not to alter it.

c. Jamison may write the report if she discloses the special relationships with the company in the report.

d. Jamison should not write the report because the two Howard officers are constructive insiders.

4. Which of the following statements clearly *conflicts* with the recommended procedures for compliance presented in CFA Institute's *Standards of Practice Handbook?*

a. Firms should disclose to clients the personal investing policies and procedures established for their employees.

b. Prior approval must be obtained for the personal investment transactions of all employees.

c. For confidentiality reasons, personal transactions and holdings should not be reported to employers unless mandated by regulatory organizations.

d. Personal transactions should be defined as including transactions in securities owned by the employee and members of his or her immediate family and transactions involving securities in which the employee has a beneficial interest.

5. Bronson provides investment advice to the board of trustees of a private university endowment fund. The trustees have provided Bronson with the fund's financial information, including planned expenditures. Bronson receives a phone call on Friday afternoon from Murdock, a prominent alumnus, requesting that Bronson fax him comprehensive financial information about the fund. According to Murdock, he has a potential contributor but needs the information that day to close the deal and cannot contact any of the trustees. Based on CFA Institute Standards, Bronson should:

a. Send Murdock the information because disclosure would benefit the client.

b. Not send Murdock the information to preserve confidentiality.

c. Send Murdock the information, provided Bronson promptly notifies the trustees.

d. Send Murdock the information because it is not material nonpublic information.

6. Miller heads the research department of a large brokerage firm. The firm has many analysts, some of whom are subject to the Code and Standards. If Miller delegates some supervisory duties, which statement best describes her responsibilities under the Code and Standards?

a. Miller's supervisory responsibilities do not apply to those subordinates who are not subject to the Code and Standards.

b. Miller no longer has supervisory responsibility for those duties delegated to her subordinates.

c. Miller retains supervisory responsibility for all subordinates despite her delegation of some duties.

d. CFA Institute Standards prevent Miller from delegating supervisory duties to subordinates.

7. Willier is the research analyst responsible for following Company X. All the information he has accumulated and documented suggests that the outlook for the firm's new products is poor, so the stock should be rated a weak hold. During lunch, however, Willier overhears a financial analyst from another firm whom he respects offer opinions that conflict with Willier's forecasts and expectations. Upon returning to his office, Willier releases a strong buy recommendation to the public. Willier:

   a. Was in full compliance with the Standards.
   b. Violated the Standards by failing to distinguish between facts and opinions in his recommendation.
   c. Violated the Standards because he did not seek approval of the change from his firm's compliance department.
   d. Violated the Standards because he did not have a reasonable and adequate basis for his recommendation.

8. An investment management firm has been hired by ETV Corporation to work on an initial public offering for the company. The firm's brokerage unit now has a sell recommendation on ETV, but the head of the investment banking department has asked the head of the brokerage unit to change the recommendation from sell to buy. According to the Standards, the head of the brokerage unit would be permitted to:

   a. Increase the recommendation by no more than one increment (in this case, to a hold recommendation).
   b. Place the company on a restricted list and give only factual information about the firm.
   c. Assign a new analyst to decide if the stock deserves a higher rating.
   d. Reassign responsibility for rating the stock to the head of the investment banking unit.

9. Albert and Tye, who recently started their own investment advisory business, have registered to take the Level III CFA examination. Albert's business card reads, "Judy Albert, CFA Level II." Tye has not put anything about the CFA designation on his business card, but promotional material that he designed for the business describes the CFA requirements and indicates that Tye participates in the CFA Program and has completed Levels I and II. According to the Standards:

   a. Albert has violated the Standards but Tye has not.
   b. Tye has violated the Standards but Albert has not.
   c. Both Albert and Tye have violated the Standards.
   d. Neither Albert nor Tye has violated the Standards.

10. Scott works for a regional brokerage firm. He estimates that Walkton Industries will increase its dividend by $1.50 a share during the next year. He realizes that this increase is contingent on pending legislation that would, if enacted, give Walkton a substantial tax break. The U.S. representative for Walkton's home district has told Scott that, although she is lobbying hard for the bill and prospects for passage look good, Congress's concern over the federal deficit could cause the tax bill to be voted down. Walkton has not made any statements regarding a change in dividend policy. Scott writes in his research report, "We expect Walkton's stock price to rise by at least $8.00 a share by the end of the year. Because the dividend will increase by $1.50 a share, the stock price gain will be fueled, in large part, by the increase in the dividend. Investors buying the stock at the current time should expect to realize a total return of at least 15 percent on the stock." Which of the following is/are *true*?

    I. Scott violated the Standards because he used material inside information.

    II. Scott violated the Standards because he failed to separate opinion from fact.

    III. Scott did not violate the Standards.

  a. I only.
  b. II only.
  c. I and II only.
  d. III only.

11. Which *one* of the following actions will *not* help to ensure the fair treatment of brokerage firm clients when a new investment recommendation is made?

  a. Limit the number of people in the firm who are aware in advance that a recommendation is to be disseminated.
  b. Distribute recommendations to institutional clients prior to individual accounts.
  c. Minimize elapsed time between the decision and the dissemination of a recommendation.
  d. Monitor the trading activities of firm personnel.

12. The mosaic theory holds that an analyst:

  a. Violates the Code and Standards if the analyst fails to have knowledge of and comply with applicable laws.
  b. Can use material public information or nonmaterial nonpublic information in the analyst's analysis.
  c. Should use all available and relevant information in support of an investment recommendation.
  d. Should distinguish between facts and opinions in research reports.

13. Jurgens is a portfolio manager. One of her firm's clients has told Jurgens that he will compensate her beyond that provided by her firm on the basis of the capital appreciation of his portfolio each year. Jurgens should:
    a. Turn down the additional compensation because it will result in conflicts with the interests of other clients' accounts.
    b. Receive permission from CFA Institute for the compensation arrangement.
    c. Obtain permission from her employer prior to accepting the compensation arrangement.
    d. Turn down the additional compensation because it will create undue pressure on her to achieve strong short-term performance.

14. One of the discretionary accounts managed by Farnsworth is the Jones Corporation employee profit-sharing plan. Jones, the company president, recently asked Farnsworth to vote the shares in the profit-sharing plan in favor of the company-nominated slate of directors and against the directors sponsored by a dissident stockholder group. Farnsworth does not want to lose this account because he directs all the account's trades to a brokerage firm that provides Farnsworth with useful information about tax-free investments. Although this information is not of value in managing the Jones Corporation account, it does help in managing several other accounts. The brokerage firm providing this information also offers the lowest commissions for trades and best execution. Farnsworth investigates the director issue, concludes that management's slate is better for the long-run performance of the firm than the dissident group's slate, and votes accordingly. Farnsworth:
    a. Violated the Standards in voting the shares in the manner requested by Jones but not in directing trades to the brokerage firm.
    b. Did not violate the Standards in voting the shares in the manner requested by Jones or in directing trades to the brokerage firm.
    c. Violated the Standards in directing trades to the brokerage firm but not in voting the shares as requested by Jones.
    d. Violated the Standards in voting the shares in the manner requested by Jones and in directing trades to the brokerage firm.

15. Brown works for an investment counseling firm. Green, a new client of the firm, is meeting with Brown for the first time. Green used another counseling firm for financial advice for years, but she has switched her account to Brown's firm. After spending a few minutes getting acquainted, Brown explains to Green that she has discovered a highly undervalued stock that offers large potential gains. She recommends that Green purchase the stock. Brown has committed a violation of the Standards. What should she have done differently?
    a. Brown should have determined Green's needs, objectives, and tolerance for risk before making a recommendation for any type of security.

b. Brown should have asked Green her reasons for changing counseling firms. If the discovery process indicated that Green had been treated unfairly at the other firm, Brown should have notified CFA Institute of any violation.

c. Brown should have thoroughly explained the characteristics of the company to Green, including the characteristics of the industry in which the company operates.

d. Brown should have explained her qualifications, including her education, training, experience, and the meaning of the CFA designation.

16. Grey recommends the purchase of a mutual fund that invests solely in long-term U.S. Treasury bonds. He makes the following statements to his clients:

    I. "The payment of the bonds is guaranteed by the U.S. government; therefore, the default risk of the bonds is virtually zero."

    II. "If you invest in the mutual fund, you will earn a 10 percent rate of return each year for the next several years based on historical performance of the stock market."

Did Grey's statements violate the CFA Institute Code and Standards?

a. Statement I and II violated the Code and Standards.
b. Only statement I violated the Code and Standards.
c. Only statement II violated the Code and Standards.
d. Neither statement violated the Code and Standards.

17. Anderb, a portfolio manager for XYZ Investment Management Company—a registered investment organization that advises investment companies and private accounts—was promoted to that position three years ago. Bates, her supervisor, is responsible for reviewing Anderb's portfolio account transactions and her required monthly reports of personal stock transactions. Anderb has been using Jonelli, a broker, almost exclusively for portfolio account brokerage transactions. For securities in which Jonelli's firm makes a market, Jonelli has been giving Anderb lower prices for personal purchases and higher prices for personal sales than Jonelli gives to Anderb's portfolio accounts and other investors. Anderb has been filing monthly reports with Bates only for those months in which she has no personal transactions, which is about every fourth month. Which of the following applies/apply?

    I. Anderb violated the Code and Standards in that she failed to disclose to her employer her personal transactions.

    II. Anderb violated the Code and Standards by breaching her fiduciary responsibility to her clients.

    III. Bates violated the Code and Standards by failing to enforce reasonable procedures for supervising and monitoring Anderb's trading for her own account.

a. I only.
b. I and II only.
c. II and III only.
d. I, II, and III.

18. Which of the following is/are a correct statement of a member or candidate's duty under the Code and Standards?

    I.   In the absence of specific applicable law or other regulatory requirements, the Code and Standards govern the member or candidate's actions.

    II. A member or candidate is required to comply only with applicable local laws, rules, regulations, or customs even though the CFA Institute Code and Standards may impose a higher degree of responsibility or a higher duty on the member or candidate.

    III. A member or candidate who trades securities in a securities market where no applicable local laws or stock exchange rules regulate the use of material nonpublic information may take investment action based on material nonpublic information.

a. I only.
b. III only.
c. II and III only.
d. I and II only.

19. Ward is scheduled to visit the corporate headquarters of Evans Industries. Ward expects to use the information obtained to complete his research report on Evans stock. Ward learns that Evans plans to pay all of Ward's expenses for the trip, including costs of meals, hotel room, and air transportation. Which of the following actions would be the *best* course for Ward to take under the Code and Standards?

a. Accept the expense-paid trip and write an objective report.
b. Pay for all travel expenses, including costs of meals and incidental items.
c. Accept the expense-paid trip but disclose the value of the services accepted in the report.
d. Write the report without taking the trip.

20. Which of the following statements is/are correct under the Code and Standards?

    I.   CFA Institute members and candidates are prohibited from undertaking independent practice in competition with their employer.

    II. Written consent from the employer is necessary to permit independent practice that could result in compensation or other benefit in competition with a member or candidate's employer.

III. Prior to leaving an employer to work for another firm or start an independent practice, members and candidates may not contact their clients to solicit their business for the new venture.

IV. Members and candidates are prohibited from making arrangements or preparations to go into a competitive business before terminating their relationship with their employer.

a. I and IV only.
b. II, III, and IV only.
c. II and III only.
d. IV only.

21. Smithers is a financial analyst with XYZ Brokerage Company. She is preparing a purchase recommendation on JNI Corporation. Which of the following situations would represent a conflict of interest for Smithers and, therefore, would have to be disclosed?

I. Smith is on retainer as a consultant to JNI.
II. XYZ holds for its own account a substantial common stock position in JNI.
III. Smith has material beneficial ownership of JNI through a family trust.
IV. Smith's brother-in-law is a supplier to JNI.

a. II and III only.
b. I and IV only.
c. I, II, and III only.
d. I, II, and IV only.

22. Michelieu tells a prospective client, "I may not have a long-term track record yet, but I'm sure that you'll be very pleased with my recommendations and service. In the three years that I've been in the business, my equity-oriented clients have averaged a total return of more than 26 percent a year." The statement is true, but Michelieu only has a few clients, and one of his clients took a large position in a penny stock (against Michelieu's advice) and realized a huge gain. This large return caused the average of all of Michelieu's clients to exceed 26 percent a year. Without this one investment, the average gain would have been 8 percent a year. Has Michelieu violated the Standards?

a. Yes, because the statement about return ignores the risk preferences of his clients.
b. No, because Michelieu is not promising that he can earn a 26 percent return in the future.
c. No, because the statement is a true and accurate description of Michelieu's track record.
d. Yes, because the statement misrepresents Michelieu's track record.

23. An investment banking department of a brokerage firm often receives material nonpublic information that could have considerable value if used in advising the firm's brokerage clients. In order to conform to the Code and Standards, which one of the following is the best policy for the brokerage firm?

    a. Permanently prohibit both purchase and sell recommendations of the stocks of clients of the investment banking department.
    b. Establish physical and informational barriers within the firm to prevent the exchange of information between the investment banking and brokerage operations.
    c. Prohibit purchase recommendations when the investment banking department has access to material nonpublic information but, in view of the fiduciary obligation to clients, allow sale of current holdings.
    d. Monitor the exchange of information between the investment banking department and the brokerage operation.

24. Stewart has been hired by Goodner Industries, Inc., to manage its pension fund. Stewart's fiduciary duty is owed to:

    a. The management of Goodner.
    b. The shareholders of Goodner.
    c. The participants and beneficiaries of Goodner's pension plan.
    d. Each of the above equally.

25. The stated purposes of Standard VI(C)–Disclosure of Referral Fees are to:

    I. Help the customer or client evaluate the full cost of the services.
    II. Help the customer or client evaluate any possible partiality shown in the recommendation of services.
    III. Help the customer or client evaluate potential conflicts of interest as a result of the participation of immediate family in transactions.

    a. I and II only.
    b. II and III only.
    c. I and III only.
    d. I, II, and III.

Exam Answers and Analysis

1. The correct answer is *b*. This question involves Standard III(B)–Fair Dealing. Smith disseminated a change in the stock recommendation to his clients but then received a request contrary to that recommendation from a client who likely had not yet received the recommendation. Prior to executing the order, Smith should take additional steps to ensure that the customer has received the change of recommendation. Answer *a* is incorrect because the client placed the order prior to receiving the recommendation and, therefore, does not have the benefit of Smith's most recent recommendation. Answer *c* is incorrect because it would result in a delay in executing an order requested by the client. Answer *d* is also incorrect; simply because the client request is contrary to the firm's recommendation does not mean a member can override a direct request by a client. After Smith contacts the client to ensure that the client received the changed recommendation, if the client still wants to place a buy order for the shares, Smith is obligated to comply with the client's directive.

2. The correct answer is *d*. This question involves Standard III(A)–Loyalty, Prudence, and Care and the specific topic of soft dollars or soft commissions. Answer *d* is the correct choice because client brokerage commissions may not be directed to pay for the investment manager's operating expenses. Answer *b* would be an incorrect choice because brokerage commissions may be directed to pay for securities research used in managing a client's portfolio. Answer *c* describes how members and candidates should determine how to use brokerage commissions: if the use is in the best interests of clients and is commensurate with the value of the services provided. Answer *a* describes a practice that is commonly referred to as "directed brokerage." Because brokerage is an asset of the client and is used to benefit the client, not the manager, such practice does not violate a duty of loyalty to the client. Members and candidates are obligated in all situations to disclose to clients their practices in the use of client brokerage commissions.

3. The correct answer is *c*. This question involves Standard VI(A)–Disclosure of Conflicts. The question establishes a conflict of interest whereby an analyst, Jamison, is asked to write a research report on a company that is a client of Jamison's employer. In addition, two directors of the company are senior officers of Jamison's employer. Both facts are conflicts of interest and must be disclosed by Jamison in her research report. Answer *d* would be incorrect because an analyst is not prevented from writing a report because of the special relationship the analyst's employer has with the company so long as that relationship is disclosed. Whether or not Jamison expresses any opinions in the report is irrelevant to her duty to disclose a conflict of interest. Not expressing opinions does not relieve the analyst of her responsibility to

disclose the special relationship between the two companies. Therefore, answer *a* is incorrect. Answer *b* is also incorrect; although an employer should not put pressure on an analyst to alter a report in any way and Jamison cannot change the report based on her employer's influence, the relationship between the two companies posing the conflict of interest must be disclosed.

4. The correct answer is *c*. This question asks about compliance procedures relating to personal investments of members and candidates. The statement in answer *c* clearly conflicts with the recommended procedures in the *Handbook*. Employers should compare personal transactions of employees with those of clients on a regular basis regardless of the existence of a requirement by a regulatory organization. Such comparisons ensure that employees' personal trades do not conflict with their duty to their clients, and the comparisons can be conducted in a confidential manner. The statement in answer *a* does not conflict with the procedures in the *Handbook*. Disclosure of such policies will give full information to clients regarding potential conflicts of interest on the part of those entrusted to manage their money. Answer *b* is incorrect because firms are encouraged to establish policies whereby employees clear personal holdings and transactions. Answer *d* describes the categories of securities that compliance procedures designed to monitor personal transactions should cover.

5. The correct answer is *b*. This question relates to Standard III(A)–Loyalty, Prudence, and Care and Standard III(E)–Preservation of Confidentiality. In this case, the member manages funds of a private endowment. Members and candidates owe a fiduciary duty to their clients, who are in this case the trustees of the fund. Bronson cannot disclose confidential financial information to anyone without the permission of the fund, regardless of whether the disclosure may benefit the fund. Therefore, answer *a* is incorrect. Answer *c* is also incorrect because Bronson must notify the fund and obtain the fund's permission before publicizing the information. Answer *d* is incorrect because, even if the information is nonmaterial, the member cannot disclose the information because it is confidential. Only if Bronson receives permission from the trustees can he disclose the information to the alumnus.

6. The correct answer is *c*. Under Standard IV(C)–Responsibilities of Supervisors, members and candidates may delegate supervisory duties to subordinates but such delegation does not relieve members or candidates of their supervisory responsibilities. As a result, answers *b* and *d* are incorrect. Moreover, whether or not Miller's subordinates are subject to the CFA Institute Code and Standards is irrelevant to her supervisory responsibilities. Therefore, answer *a* is incorrect.

7. The correct answer is *d*. This question relates to Standard V(A)–Diligence and Reasonable Basis. Willier's action in changing the recommendation based on the opinion of another financial analyst is not an adequate basis for the recommendation. Answer *a* is thus incorrect. So is answer *b* because, although it is true that members and candidates must distinguish between facts and opinions in recommendations, the question does not illustrate a violation of that nature. Answer *c* is incorrect; whether or not a member or candidate has to seek approval from the firm of a change in a recommendation is a matter of policy set by the firm; the Standards do not require that members and candidates seek such approval. If the opinion overheard by Willier had sparked him to conduct additional research and investigation that justified a change of opinion, then a changed recommendation would be appropriate.

8. The correct answer is *b*. This question relates to Standard I(B)–Independence and Objectivity. When asked to change a recommendation on a company stock to gain business for the firm, the head of the brokerage unit must refuse in order to maintain his independence and objectivity in making the recommendation. He must not yield to pressure by the firm's investment banking department. To avoid the appearance of a conflict of interest, the firm should discontinue issuing recommendations about the company. Answer *a* is incorrect; changing the recommendation in any manner that is contrary to the analyst's opinion violates the duty to maintain independence and objectivity. Answer *c* is incorrect because merely assigning a new analyst to decide if the stock deserves a higher rating will not address the conflict of interest. Answer *d* would actually exacerbate the conflict of interest.

9. The correct answer is *a*. Standard VI(C)–Reference to CFA Institute, the CFA Designation, and the CFA Program is the subject of this question. The reference on Albert's business card implies that there is a "CFA Level II" designation; Tye merely indicates in promotional material that he is participating in the CFA Program and has completed Levels I and II. Candidates may not imply that there is some sort of partial designation earned after passing one level of the CFA examination. Therefore, Albert has violated Standard VI(C). Candidates may communicate that they are participating in the CFA Program, however, and may state the levels that they have completed. Therefore, Tye has not violated Standard II(A).

10. The correct answer is *b*. This question relates to Standard V(B)–Communication with Clients and Prospective Clients. Scott has issued a research report stating that he expects the price of Walkton Industries stock to rise by $8 a share "because the dividend will increase" by $1.50 per share. He makes this statement knowing that the dividend will increase only if Congress enacts certain legislation, an uncertain prospect. By stating that the dividend will increase, Scott failed to separate fact from opinion. Therefore,

statement II is correct. The information regarding passage of legislation is not material nonpublic information because it is conjecture and it is not clear that the U.S. Representative gave Scott her opinion on the passage of the legislation in confidence. She could be offering this opinion to anyone who asks. Statement I is incorrect, as is statement III.

11. The correct answer is *b*. This question, which relates to Standard III(B)–Fair Dealing, tests the knowledge of the procedures that will assist members and candidates to treat clients fairly when making investment recommendations. The steps listed in *a*, *c*, and *d* will all help ensure the fair treatment of clients. Answer *b*, distributing recommendations to institutional clients before distributing them to individual accounts, discriminates among clients based on size and class of assets and is a violation of Standard III(B).

12. The correct answer is *b*. This question deals with Standard II(A)–Material Nonpublic Information. The mosaic theory states that an analyst may use material public information or nonmaterial nonpublic information in creating a larger picture than shown by any individual piece of information and the conclusions the analyst reaches become material only after the pieces are assembled. Answers *a*, *c*, and *d* are accurate statements relating to the Code and Standards but do not describe the mosaic theory.

13. The correct answer is *c*. This question involves Standard IV(B)–Additional Compensation Arrangements. The arrangement described in the question, whereby Jurgens would be compensated, based on the account's performance, beyond that provided by her firm, is not a violation of the Standards so long as Jurgens discloses the arrangement in writing to her employer and obtains permission from her employer prior to entering into the arrangement. Answer *a* is incorrect; although the private compensation arrangement could conflict with the interests of other clients, members and candidates may enter into such agreements so long as they have disclosed the arrangements to their employer and obtained permission for the arrangement from their employer. Answer *d* is also incorrect, this potential conflict can be managed through disclosure. Answer *b* is incorrect because members and candidates are not required to receive permission from CFA Institute for such arrangements.

14. The correct answer is *b*. This question Standard III(A)–Loyalty, Prudence, and Care, specifically, a member or candidate's responsibility for voting proxies and the use of client brokerage. According to the facts stated in the question, Farnsworth did not violate Standard III(A). Although the company president asked Farnsworth to vote the shares of the Jones Corporation profit-sharing plan a certain way, Farnsworth investigated the issue and concluded, independently, the best way to vote. Therefore, even though his decision coincided with the wishes of the company president, Farnsworth

is not in violation of his fiduciary responsibility to his clients. In this case, the participants and the beneficiaries of the profit-sharing plan are the clients, not the company's management. Had Farnsworth not investigated the issue or had he yielded to the president's wishes and voted for a slate of directors that he had determined was not in the best interest of the company, Farnsworth would have violated his fiduciary responsibility to the beneficiaries of the plan. In addition, because the brokerage firm provides the lowest commissions and best execution for securities transactions, Farnsworth has met his fiduciary duties to the client in using this brokerage firm. It does not matter that the brokerage firm also provides research information that is not useful for the account generating the commission, because Farnsworth is not paying extra money of the client's for that information.

15. The correct answer is *a*. In this question, Brown is providing investment recommendations before making inquiries about the client's financial situation, investment experience, or investment objectives. Brown is thus violating Standard III(C)–Suitability. As for answer *b*, why the client changed investment firms might be useful information, but it is not the only information the member needs to provide suitable investment recommendations, and Brown is under no obligation to notify CFA Institute of any violation of the Code and Standards other than her own. Answers *c* and *d* provide examples of information members and candidates should discuss with their clients at the outset of the relationship, but these answers do not constitute a complete list of those factors. Answer *a* is the best answer.

16. The correct answer is *c*. This question involves Standard I(C)–Misrepresentation. Statement I is a factual statement that discloses to clients and prospects accurate information about the terms of the investment instrument. Statement II, which guarantees a specific rate of return for a mutual fund, is an opinion stated as a fact and, therefore, violates Standard I(C). If statement II were rephrased to include a qualifying statement, such as "in my opinion, investors may earn...," it would not be in violation of the Standards.

17. The correct answer is *d*. This question involves three Standards. Anderb, the portfolio manager, has been obtaining lower prices for her personal securities transactions than she gets for her clients, which is a breach of Standard III(A)–Loyalty, Prudence, and Care. In addition, she violated Standard I(D)–Misconduct, by failing to adhere to company policy and hiding her personal transactions from her firm. Anderb's supervisor, Bates, violated Standard IV(C)–Responsibilities of Supervisors; although the company had requirements for reporting personal trading, Bates failed to adequately enforce those procedures. Therefore, statements I, II, and III are all correct.

18. The correct answer is *a*. This question relates to Standard I(A)–Knowledge of the Law, specifically, global application of the Code and Standards. Members and candidates who practice in multiple jurisdictions may be subject to various securities laws and regulations. If applicable law is more strict than the requirements of the Code and Standards, members and candidates must adhere to applicable law; otherwise, members and candidates must adhere to the Code and Standards. Therefore, statement I is correct. Statement II is incorrect because members and candidates must adhere to the higher standard set by the Code and Standards if local applicable law is less strict. Statement III is incorrect because when no applicable law exists, members and candidates are required to adhere to the Code and Standards, and the Code and Standards prohibit the use of material nonpublic information.

19. The correct answer is *b*. The best course of action under Standard I(B)–Independence and Objectivity is to avoid a conflict of interest whenever possible. Therefore, paying for all expenses is the correct answer. Answer *c* details a course of action in which the conflict would be disclosed, but the solution is not as appropriate as avoiding the conflict of interest. Answer *a* would not be the best course because it would not remove the appearance of a conflict of interest; even though the report would not be affected by the reimbursement of expenses, it could appear to be. Answer *d* is not appropriate because, by failing to take advantage of close inspection of the company, Ward would not be using all the information available in completing his report.

20. The correct answer is *c*. Under Standard IV(A)–Duties to Employer: Loyalty, members and candidates may undertake independent practice that may result in compensation or other benefit in competition with their employer so long as they obtain consent from their employer. Statements II and III are consistent with Standard III(B). Statement I is not correct because the Standards do not include a complete prohibition against undertaking independent practice. Statement IV is also incorrect because the Standards allow members and candidates to make arrangements or preparations to go into competitive business so long as those arrangements do not interfere with their duty to their current employer.

21. The correct answer is *c*. This question involves Standard VI(A)–Disclosure of Conflicts. Statements I, II, and III describe conflicts of interest for Smithers or her firm that would have to be disclosed. Statement I describes an employment relationship between the analyst and the company that is the subject of the recommendation. Statement II describes the beneficial interest of the analyst's employer in the company's stock, and statement III describes the analyst's own beneficial interest in the company stock. In statement IV, the relationship between the analyst and the company through a relative is so tangential that it does not create a conflict of interest necessitating disclosure.

22. The correct answer is *d*. This question relates to Standard I(C)–Misrepresentation. Although Michelieu's statement regarding the total return of his client's accounts on average may be technically true, it is misleading because the majority of the gain resulted from one client's large position taken against Michelieu's advice. Therefore, this statement misrepresents the investment performance the member is responsible for. He has not taken steps to present a fair, accurate, and complete presentation of performance. Answer *c* is thus incorrect. Answer *b* is incorrect because although Michelieu is not guaranteeing future results, his words are still a misrepresentation of his performance history. Answer *a* is incorrect because failing to disclose the risk preferences of clients does not make a statement misleading and is not a violation of the Standards in this context.

23. The correct answer is *b*. The best policy to prevent violation of Standard II(A)–Material Nonpublic Information is the establishment of "fire walls" within a firm to prevent exchange of insider information. The physical and informational barrier of a fire wall between the investment banking department and the brokerage operation prevents the investment banking department from providing information to analysts on the brokerage side who may be writing recommendations regarding a company stock. Prohibiting recommendations of the stock of companies that are clients of the investment banking department is an alternative, but answer *a* states that this prohibition would be permanent, which is not the best answer. Once an offering is complete and the material nonpublic information obtained by the investment banking department becomes public, resuming publishing recommendations on the stock is not a violation of the Code and Standards because the information of the investment banking department no longer gives the brokerage operation an advantage in writing the report. Answer *c* is incorrect; whether or not a fiduciary duty is owed to clients does not override the prohibition against use of material nonpublic information. Answer *d* is incorrect because no exchange of information should be occurring between the investment banking department and the brokerage operation, so monitoring of such exchanges is not an effective compliance procedure for preventing the use of material nonpublic information.

24. The correct answer is *c*. Under Standard III(A)–Loyalty, Prudence, and Care, members and candidates who manage a company's pension funds owe a fiduciary duty to the participants and beneficiaries of the plan, not the management of the company or the company shareholders.

25. The correct answer is *a*. Statements I and II give the two primary reasons listed in the *Standards of Practice Handbook* for disclosing referral fees to clients. The purpose given in statement III is not a primary consideration.

A

B

C

O

P

S

V

W